More Family Jewels

Further Explorations in Male Genitorture

First Edition

Hardy Haberman

More Family Jewels

Further Explorations in Male Genitorture

First Edition

Published by The Nazca Plains Corporation
Las Vegas, Nevada
2007

ISBN: 978-1-934625-09-5

Published by

The Nazca Plains Corporation ®
4640 Paradise Rd, Suite 141
Las Vegas NV 89109-8000

Illustrations, Issac Tucker
Cover, © Vova Pomortzeff - FOTOLIA
Art Director, Blake Stephens

Acknowledgements

Each of us is a living history of all the people we have known. It is to those people in the leather community I have been privileged to know that I owe a debt. From my first forays into leather back in the mid-1970's to the present I continue to learn. Many times my instructors were unaware they were teaching me, but you can learn in a lot of ways.

I would like to specially thank Tony DeBlaze whose delight and expertise I was privileged to observe. He was always willing to give me suggestions and advice, just as he was to anyone in the leather community. Tony will be missed. I would also like to thank my close friends, Jim Richards, Mark Frazier, Daddy Ron Hertz, Jim Hawkins and Parker Perry, and Ms Twisted for their continued advice and insight. I owe a debt to Issac Tucker for his excellent illustrations in this book and to his boy Brenton who has served as enthusiastic "crash test dummy" for several of my experiments.

Last, but not least I wish to thank the Dallas leatherfolk and the fine members of the National Leather Association International for their continued support and work on behalf of the entire leather community.

Dedication

This book is dedicated to my boy Patrick,
whose patience and love are worth more than any jewels.

More Family Jewels

Further Explorations in Male Genitorture

Hardy Haberman

Contents

Foreword

I got clamps in my pants and I need to dance. (Or: CBT will make a sex machine outta y'all.)

Own up to it. You've seen the cover of this book or maybe flipped through a couple of the stories and you can barely contain the urge to get to the juicy stuff. Maybe you've already absorbed Hardy Haberman's original *The Family Jewels* and were starving for more. But maybe you're not. Why, you may ask, do I want somebody to get anything remotely painful down *there*?!? I mean, they're a perfectly good set of testes and I happen to be quite attached to them, you say.

Good question. Perfectly reasonable, for that matter. After all, one does not want to go to the play party a baritone and come home a falsetto. Hardy once described himself to me as a "Pain Technician," and I can certainly vouch for the veracity of that claim. I have seen him in action, and he can definitely make you dance. I also know that everyone went home afterwards with big canary-eating grins on their faces, including Hardy. Keep that in mind as you start perusing these real-life narratives of men whose balls went bump in the night.

You see, those lovely little orbs are resilient critters. Should you be the one letting your fingers do the pinching or the man for whom the pain is being brought, chances are you'll discover just how much you'll enjoy getting that sensation. Control, power, submission, manhood; all centered around that itty-bitty region on such a small percentage of body space. Think of that for a moment…all those sensitive, tingly, nerve endings on a length of skin you can get your thumb and forefinger around. And up. And down. Lube, repeat, rinse. Because if you're reading this, you've probably given more than a passing fantasy over to the thrills of Cock and Ball Torture.

After all, how many TV shows and movies tantalize us with the exciting threat? Everyone from James Bond to Jack Bauer has hooked our viewing to scenes of men getting their privates worked over. What episode of whatever configuration of *Funniest Home Videos* would be complete without Uncle Charlie taking one for the team (from the flying baseball, the family dog or the garden rake)? It not only makes us excited, it makes us laugh. Jack Fritscher once told me, all great sex is comedy. Even the kinky variety.

The other great thing about CBT play is the simplicity of it all. Who needs Torquemada when you have Ace Hardware? For that matter, your local Staples? Go buy yourself some rubber bands (you'll see that in the "On Target" chapter) or even a bag of clothespins, and you've got an instant starter kit. As Hardy explains throughout this book, you don't have be a member of The Spanish Inquisition or the earner of a six figure income to get a good scene off the ground. CBT is one of many forms of SM easily done on a miniscule budget. It hardly even needs to be threatening. You can get a rise out of your partner with a Depeche Mode CD, bootlaces, an ice-cube, cherry gelatin and a squeaky dog-toy (don't ask). You're going to love what Hardy does with some old, cheap forceps. It's Erotica on Two Dollars a Day.

You've got *More Family Jewels* in your hands. You're now among friends. You're friends just happen to be kinky and have a fascination with tormented sex organs. If you've ever given thought to letting someone get their fingers across the folds of your scrotum (or vice-versa), you've come to the right place.

Read on, no matter what your experience level. Take notes, experiment. That valuable spot between your ears is going to start dreaming up all sorts of excitement for the smaller valuable spot in a somewhat lower region. You're going to be hollering "I feel GOOD!" before you know it.

Tim Brough

Tim Brough is the author of *Black Gloves White Magic, Sgt Vlengles' Revenge, First Hand: An Erotic Guide to Fisting* and *Skin Tight: A Guide to Rubbermen, Macho Fetish and Fantasy.* He has really nice, hairless balls. His website is www.TimBrough. com.

Preface

When I wrote my first book, *Family Jewels, a Guide to Male Genitorture and Torment*, I had no idea how many people would be interested in the topic. I had assumed that cock and ball torture was a fairly specialized BDSM scene and would only be of interest to dedicated players, and most of them gay men. I was pleasantly surprised to find that my readers were about equally split between women and men, and the thirst for information about CBT seemed bottomless. (No pun intended.)

Since then I have done hundreds of workshops and lectures on the subject and find my audiences more diverse than I could ever imagine. Much of the interest comes from people who had never considered CBT until they attended one of my workshops. I guess we both got surprises. To watch the faces of men and women when their imaginations kick in during a demonstration is remarkable. Their sex lives are opened up to the possibilities of something new and exciting.

My imagination has been expanded as well. I get lots of suggestions and ideas given to me during the workshops. These come in the form of concepts for new toys, new ways to use old ones, and new scenarios in which to include CBT. I decided that these gifts along with the new ideas and techniques I have learned since the first book would be a good starting place for further writing on the subject.

I have written this book as a collection of stories. I had a lot of positive comments about the stories in my last book because they give real world examples of how to use the techniques in a scene. I sincerely hope that this book will inspire the reader to break out of old sexual ruts and try new experiences.

The stories contained here are drawn from my personal experience and from the vast number of CBT scenes I have witnessed. I have done a little rearranging of the names and locations to assure my friends of they privacy. That said, a few people might be able to still recognize a persona or location that seems familiar. If you do, think of it like discovering a magician's secret tricks. It's more fun when people don't know how it's done.

Additionally, I have tried to make the necessary information regarding the safety of specific techniques obvious in the stories. I have always been very concerned with the safety of the activities in which I engage. In the realm of cock and ball torture, disregarding reasonable safety precautions can have disastrous consequences.

I also urge anyone interested in becoming more skilled at CBT to find a knowledgeable mentor who can show you the ropes. They don't have to be a renowned expert, just someone who you have seen play and can trust. Ask others in the community to assist you in finding an appropriate mentor. I have found people in the leather/fetish/BDSM community are almost always willing to share what they know and to recommend someone with experience. If you are shy about asking for help, remember it is a compliment to be asked to share your knowledge. I have rarely found rejection from people I have asked for information. Most are happy to share and teach what they know.

The great thing I have found in my years in the leather/kink community is that I never stop learning. New ideas and twists are around every corner, and the real joy for me is exploring. This quest keeps things spicy in my life and constantly reminds me that I don't know it all. That humility is one of the greatest gifts I have received. I am reminded that we are all sexual explorers, and like any explorer we often take wrong turns or find ourselves in blind alleyways. However, often we manage to find treasures and those are the best jewels we can collect.

Speaking the Same Language – A Brief Glossary

In the kinky world, we use a lot of jargon that could be easily misinterpreted by those unfamiliar with our language. For that matter different areas of the country use terms to mean different things. So in the interest of better communication and to avoid any confusion here are a few terms I use in the book.

CBT – this is not computer based training and if that is what you think it means, you have bought the wrong book. It stands for cock and ball torture, though not everything in this venue is painful. I sometimes call it CBP or cock and ball play which, for me is a more accurate acronym.

BDSM – an acronym most often representing Bondage, Discipline (BD) and Sadomasochism (SM). Some people also include Dominance and Submission (DS) giving the middle two letters different meaning. When I use it I am always referring to consensual activity between adults. These terms and or their derivatives will appear often as a short hand to avoid the inevitable tongue twisting that comes from spelling them out fully.

GLBT – (Not a sandwich!) Another acronym standing for Gay Lesbian Bisexual Transgender. Again it avoids overly verbose sentences.

The Scene – I use this term to speak of the leather/fetish/BDSM community. It also includes pretty much all kinky activities included in the leather/fetish area.

A Scene – a specific play activity. Scenes usually last from a few minutes to several hours. Some even last a very long time, days or weeks. These are not the same as a relationship like that of a Daddy/boy or Master/slave.

Lifestyle – I loath this word and will use it only in quotations. It refers to the BDSM scene as well, but I personally do not consider what I do a lifestyle, it is my life. Lifestyle, to me is indicative of a trendy passing fad, and my kink is not a passing fad.

Kink – A term referring to sexual activity that is outside the most ordinary and unadventurous kind. It can also refer to almost all activities in the BDSM scene.

Kinky – adjective referring to the activities described above and the texture of my pubic hair.

Vanilla – referring to a person who is not part of the BDSM or kink community. I understand it also can be a flavor of ice cream.

Leather – sometimes referring to a fetish for leather garments and accessories, also referring to BDSM activities in general.

Leatherman – a male member of the Leather or BDSM Community. The term comes from the gay community but is now used to refer to any male identified individual in the scene. It has no role connotation of dominance or submission. Traditionally, a Leatherman wears leather: chaps, vests, boots, harnesses, etc. These are all symbols as well as fetish clothing that can immediately indicate his preferences. The image of the Leatherman has been iconized by artists such as Tom of Finland.

Leatherwoman – same as above but with alternate plumbing.

Top – The dominant participant in SM activity. Most often used by gay men to indicate who is in control of the scene or who is in the dominant role in a sexual coupling. In text this term is usually capitalized to indicate the dominant role.

bottom – Referring to the passive or submissive role in an SM scene. A person can "bottom" in a scene without being submissive. Bottoming is an activity that would include receiving the effects of an activity such as flogging or spanking. In text this term is usually not capitalized to indicate the submissive role.

Dom or Domme – The masculine and feminine terms used for a person in a dominant role in a DS scene. (both are pronounced "dahm", Domme is a French derivative and the "me" ending is silent. This is a pet peeve for me since many people pronounce the feminine word as "dah-mey". Sacré bleu!)

sub or subbie – referring to the person playing a submissive role in a DS scene. The diminutive "subbie" is used often by Dommes in reference to their partners as a term of endearment.

Daddy – Not your father! Daddies are leathermen who play the role of protective and sometimes disciplining parent. Many people play "Daddy/boy" scenes. These have nothing to do with child abuse, they are roles taken on by the partners and are far too involved to go into here. Daddies can be either straight or gay or bisexual. Some lesbians assume a Daddy role as well. Confused? Just wait.

boy – the other half of a Daddy/boy relationship. Boys are submissive, but unlike slaves, most boys are not owned property. They are sometimes feisty, mischievous and playful. They may wear a collar or they may not. The whole boy culture is far too big an issue to get into here. Suffice it to say, they are in reality adults not children!

boi – originally started by black leathermen as a term for their boys. The word "boy" had too many racist overtones and so they took to changing the spelling. (This is the story I have learned, there are surely others.) Also a term used by women who identify as boys in their relationships or play.

Mommy – female equivalent to a Daddy. So far I have not met a man who identified as a Mommy, but the world is a very large place.

girl – female equivalent to the boy role.

gurl – expletive used in the gay community to mean anything from "hello" to "Oh my God, what were you thinking wearing that mess you got on!"

Master – You will see this honorific thrown around a lot in the BDSM community. It is a title used for a person who has a "slave". I prefer to reserve that title for the slave to use for his or her Master. That said, there are people who are known as "Master (insert name here)" in the community and it serves as their scene name. A few people are commonly called Master by the community and this usually denotes their standing as a respected member of that community. Again, it's all very complex and could be the subject of another book by itself.

slave – a person who voluntarily takes on the role of someone "owned" by another. Many times slaves and Masters have contracts that spell out their obligations and property rights specifically, other times it is a casual relationship. The Master/slave community has grown recently and is already the subject of several good books on the subject.

Play – the activities that take place during a BDSM session. Flogging, spanking, bondage, CBT, etc. Originally these were referred to as "work" by early gay leathermen but the term has fallen out of favor.

Player – any participant in the BDSM/Leather/Fetish activities. People involved in a scene are referred to as players.

Scene Name – for kinky people who are in the closet or feel they must remain anonymous, many use assumed names in the community. This is a source of both endless amusement and endless confusion. What started as simple nom de plumes have become a morass of odd names and titles. Though I personally have never used a scene name, I respect people who do, and try to call them whatever they want in public.

Dungeon – (also referred to as a playspace) a space designed for BDSM activities. This can be a room in an individuals house that is reserved for play, or a large space open to members of a club or the public at large. Public dungeons are not really "public". In almost all cases for legal reasons, they are open to members only or guests of members. Whenever I speak of public play, I am referring to play in this kind of space. Anyone entering a dungeon knows that they will be seeing BDSM activities. A dungeon is a consensual space.

Safeword – a prearranged signal or word that a bottom can use to let the Top know he or she has reached their limit. It can also be used when a bottom panics or needs to communicate with the Top regarding safety, comfort or other information. Many people use the traffic light colors for safe words.

> *Red* = stop!
> *Yellow* = getting close to the limit.
> *Green* = what the hell are you waiting for?

Safe, sane and consensual – a motto first used to describe what members of the BDSM community do in private. It has become a guideline for BDSM play that helps protect everyone involved. As with almost every aspect of BDSM, the terms are somewhat subjective. Here is my take on them:

> *Safe* - an activity that does not present a risk to the health of the players.

Sane - all activities that are undertaken in a reasonably sane state of mind.
Consensual - all activities involve the full informed consent of everyone involved.
(This is why a Dungeon is a consensual space, even though I may refer to it as a public playspace.)

This is not intended to be a definitive glossary of terms but it should be sufficient to give someone who is not familiar with our activities a basic understanding of the terminology. Also, this is the way I use these terms. Others may differ on their definitions, but that is a whole different discussion.

If all this is a bit too much for you, put the book down for a while and then pick it up once you recover. For many people the first time they are exposed to the BDSM/Leather/fetish world they are overwhelmed. It's understandable. BDSM challenges the whole paradigm of modern life. It looks at the world and relationships in a vastly different and frank way and that can be unsettling. The good news is it can also be one of the most freeing experiences you can ever have.

Safety and the Nuts & Bolts of Cock and Ball Torture

I am not a doctor, though I may play one in the dungeon. Because of that, I strongly suggest taking any serious medical questions you might have about the safety of a particular activity to your physician. If you do not feel comfortable talking with him or her about these kinds of things, perhaps you need a different doctor. There are lots of qualified professionals out there who will understand, sometimes it just takes a little shopping around to find them.

I can, however, give you some general advice on how to play safely that I have learned. This isn't rocket science, it's just common sense.

First, don't break your toys. The toys I am talking about are not those you buy, but those you or your play partner were born with. Don't do anything that is going to cause permanent damage to the penis or testicles. If you have a question if something will cause permanent damage, err on the side of caution. Get qualified medical advice if necessary, and that does not mean after the fact!

Second, make sure everything you do has been negotiated. This does not mean you have to have a list with lengthy details of exactly what will happen in a scene for your partner to sign off on. It means that you and whoever you are going to play with have a reasonable idea of what may be involved and what general direction the scene will go. It also means having some sort of safeword or signal that either player can use to end the scene for whatever reason necessary. Tops can have safewords, too!

The negotiation can be very simple, especially if you are known for a specific kind of scene. You simply ask the bottom if they know what kind of scenes you like. If they answer in the affirmative, and they can tell you a little of what they expect, you are going to be fine. If either the Top or bottom cannot talk reasonably about their expectations in a scene, then it's probably a good idea to not play at all.

Third, and this is important. Be aware of any health problems prior to the scene starting. For example if you are playing with a man who has Asthma, be sure he has any needed medications available. Sometimes while playing, some bottoms hyperventillate and that may trigger an asthma attack. Having a rescue bronchodilator handy can save a trip to the hospital. A person with a communicable disease such as HIV or any other blood borne pathogen will change the way you play with them. Doing a piercing scene with an HIV positive person will carry a much higher risk than a person whom is not. In the case of a piercing scene, the actual play will be he same, since any scene involving blood or any invasive activity should be treated with the same precautions.

Fourth, maintain communication during the scene. This doesn't mean you have to chat with your play partner throughout the scene, it means that you get feedback from them through verbal or physical means so you know how your partner is processing the sensations. Some people have obvious enough body language that you can read them just by watching their bodies. Others you have to talk to and coax information from regarding the scene. I often set up a communication protocol before the scene with my play partner. I will have them address me as "Sir" as long as the scene is working for them, They are to answer any question with the addition of the word "Sir." If things are getting too intense I tell them to address me by my name. That way they know we can talk about what is going on without ending the scene. Verbal communication from some bottoms comes in the form of the noises they make. If they are cursing and smart-mouthing, it probably means they are having a good time and want more. If they suddenly become uncommunicative or their cursing turns to whimpers, it's probably time to check in with them.

Finally, let me say a few words about the term torture. What we do in the dungeon and in our play as leatherfolk is not real torture. We may emulate the kinds of things that have been done historically to torture victims, but in reality our play is generally safe, sane and consensual. What we do is, in the end, for the pleasure of both parties, otherwise it might be categorized as abuse.

Though the person receiving the sensations may feel genuine pain, it is how they process it that matters. If it is pain that is welcomed it will be perceived differently than pain that is unwelcome. To one person an unexpected slap on the back may be painful, to another it can be a comforting sign of friendship. Sensations are in the brain of the beholder. Torture to you may be tantalizing to me.

Pain

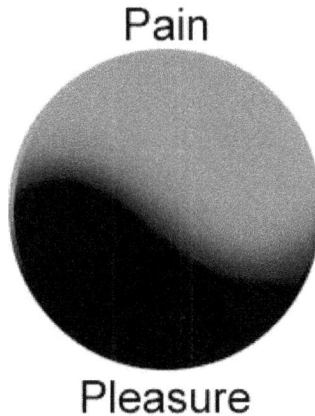

Pleasure

Why is this important? To understand how pain works I find it useful to think of pain and pleasure as a continuum. One flows seamlessly into the other and vice versa. To understand the pain/ pleasure continuum in a graphic way, consider a circle. The top arc represents pain and the bottom arc represents pleasure. The dividing line between the two arcs is not fixed, rather it moves constantly because of many of the factors already discussed. To try to fix a specific point on the circumference of the circle is equally difficult, so we can only find general areas that can be clearly identified as absolute pain or pleasure.

It is perhaps no accident that the Taoist symbol *taijitu*, the yin and yang, looks like this circle. It represents the passive and active, the dark and light, the feminine and masculine. To see this, as a dichotomy with one force being superior to the other is a Western view, the Eastern view is that each exists as a cyclical process, integral to each other and are interdependent. All SM is based on the give and take, the dichotomy of pain and pleasure and the absolute interdependence of both.

This dance of pain and pleasure really becomes evident in CBT. The physical and psychological factors that come into play in a man's genitals make them a prime place for powerful activity. The vast array of nerve endings and receptors present make a man's genitals one of the most sensitive parts of his body, and yet they are resilient enough to withstand the physical stresses of sex without damage. Beyond their importance as an erogenous zone, men often invest a lot of their self-esteem and even personality in their cock and balls. If you don't believe this, ask a few guys you know if they have names for their penis. You will find a surprising number do. Further proof of the power of the penis is even present in our humor. How many times have you heard the expression "thinking with his dick"? Funny, but there is truth to that joke as well.

Because of these factors the pain/pleasure continuum can really work to the benefit of a CBT scene. With experimentation you will find that something you once may have thought of as painful becomes a real turn on. The first time I put on a cock ring, I found it kind of restrictive and a bit painful when I got an erection. Today, I absolutely love the tight feeling of a cock ring. I feel it enhances the sensations in my penis and generally is a whole lot of fun. Again, it is all in our perception.

Common Sense

Anyone undertaking any activity described in this book, does so at his or her own risk. I am assuming we are all adults here, and as adults we are responsible for our own actions. Just because you read a story about someone jumping off a cliff and surviving without a scratch, you don't go out and try to duplicate that experience. If you do, you are in serious need of therapy, or will be once you crash to the ground and break several bones. In this age of *Jackass* on television, there are going to be people who will try anything and often without any consideration of the consequences. Every action has consequences! Use common sense and safety precautions whenever doing anything that has a potential for physical or psychological harm.

Pouring Piss from a Boot

The campsite was pretty plush as campsites go. We had a fully functional bathroom and shower facility just a couple of hundred feet from the tent, and the club had provided lots of food and drink for the weekend. The only rustic aspect to the whole affair was the tent and the uncomfortable cots we slept in. Still it was the great outdoors and we were miles from prying eyes on a private site owned jointly by our club and a couple of dozen others. Because it was so remote, it meant we could shout, yell and do just about anything within reason with each other and not be interrupted.

That privacy made some serious SM play outdoors even more attractive. I love playing outside. The sun, the air and the freedom of the great outdoors is an aphrodisiac to me. It also inspires some of my best scenes, and today was promising to be one of them.

I had met the two boys at an earlier event back in town, and they had been eager to bottom for me in a scene. Since they were both ex-marines I figured some sort of military scenario would work both for them and for me. I love a man in or out of a uniform.

The two eager men showed up at my tent as agreed promptly at 1:00pm. The sun was high in the sky, but the temperatures had not yet reached the sweltering peaks they would later in the summer.

"Pigs reporting for duty, Sir. As requested, Sir," Kevin barked, letting me know of their arrival.

Bob and Kevin looked like a pair of bookends. Both were still lean and muscular from their days in the service, though they had been civilians now for almost three years. They still sported the jar-head high and tight haircuts from the corps and knowing my uniform fetish, they arrived in freshly pressed BDUs. The gray camouflage patterns on their uniforms reminded me that these guys had last been deployed in an urban environment, somewhere in Iraq. I think knowing that made me even more determined to give them a memorable scene; they deserved it after the hell they had been through.

I walked out of my tent and slowly strolled around the handsome men standing at attention before me. As I completed the circle, I stopped and turned to face them.

"So are you pigs ready for this?" I growled.

"Sir, yes Sir!"

I smiled in acknowledgement and then turned my back on them.

"If you were really ready, you'd be out of those damn uniforms and buck naked except for your socks and boots."

I remained with my back to them and listened as I heard a flurry of clothing rustle and buckles unsnapping. Once things were quiet, I turned to face them. Before me stood a pair of gorgeous naked men, both a little under 6 feet tall with their arms clasped behind their backs and standing at attention.

I nodded approvingly, "Now that's one hundred percent better!"

"Sir, yes Sir!"

I was going to really like this. I reached inside the tent and pulled out my pack. Inside I had all the toys and tools I would need for the scene.

"Now, pigs, you fall in behind me."

With that I turned and walked toward a stand of trees. The two boys followed in lock step, parading naked and proud through the campground to the delight of the other men at the event. The nice thing for me was not only playing with them, but also having them following me. It's always nice to be followed around by such tasty eye-candy.

Once we arrived at the trees, I told them to stand at attention, facing the rest of the campsite. Might as well give the other guys something nice to look at while I got ready.

I opened my pack and pulled out several long leather belts. I have found these come in handy for bondage, and being a rather lazy Top, I like them because they are quick and easy. I also brought some black nylon woven rope and a couple of ball stretchers with attachments for hanging weights. The last tools out of the pack were four pulleys I had picked up at the hardware store. These were the kind with two wheels on each mounted side by side. By using these kinds of pulleys, you can lift heavier objects with less effort, or in my case make a smaller weight have a greater effect.

I had stopped the guys between a couple of trees I scoped out earlier. These would be perfect for the scene I had in mind. The straight trunks would make great spots to anchor the boys to, and the low hanging limbs would serve to as a place to hang the pulleys.

I reached in my pocket and pulled out a dry erase marker. Walking around so I faced the two men, I noticed that their cocks were standing at attention almost as stiffly as they were.

"Just so I can tell you two pigs apart," I spat, "I'm gonna mark you. That way both you and I will know which pig I am talking to."

I uncapped the marker and proceeded to mark Kevin's shaved chest with large black letters: "Pig #1".

"You are Pig number one, understand boy?"

"Sir, yes Sir. Pig number one at your service, Sir." Kevin shouted.

I noticed a few of the other men in the campsite starting to move closer to get a good look. That was no problem for me, I enjoy having an audience sometimes, and this was one of those times.

Moving to Bob I marked his slightly furry chest in a similar way. "Pig #2."

"You are Pig number 2, understand boy?"

"Sir, yes Sir. Pig number two at your service, Sir."

By now, my cock was starting to stand at attention as well, but it was safely tucked inside my jeans though it was feeling a little uncomfortable.

I walked behind them and took a piece of rope about 8 feet long and tossed one end over the tree branch. Giving it a couple of tugs to test the strength of the branch I then attached two of the pulleys to the rope and tied it off in a loop. They hung about 6 feet from the ground, just the right height for what I had in mind.

Now I walked back to the boys. "Pig number 1, get your ass over to that tree, back against it facing the other tree!" I shouted it right in Kevin's face, and I saw him respond like I would have imagined he did when he was in basic training. His chin tucked back and his body stiffened.

"Sir, yes Sir"

He flew to the tree and stood rigidly against the rough bark. I then turned to Bob.

"Pig number two, get over to the other tree facing Pig number 1 and make it snappy!"

Bob did make it snappy and was flat against the tree in an instant. I moved behind him and passed one of the leather belts around him and the tree, pulling it tight around his chest I bound him to the tree. I took a second belt and did the same around his thighs, leaving enough slack to allow his knees to bend slightly. The rough tree bark kept the belts from sliding down. The last belt went around his waist, pinning his arms to his sides.

After checking to be sure that he was safely anchored, I did the same with Kevin. Soon, both boys were secure, facing each other across a space of about 6 feet.

Now I took another piece of rope, this one about 20 feet long and threaded it through one of the pulleys hanging from the branch between them. I proceed to thread it through another pulley, then back through the hanging one and again through the extra one. This created the mechanical means for the scene, a block and tackle. The rope, threaded twice through the two pulleys would act to amplify any force exerted on the rope. High school physics pays off again!

I did the same with the other hanging pulley, making an identical block and tackle. Out of the corner of my eyes I watched

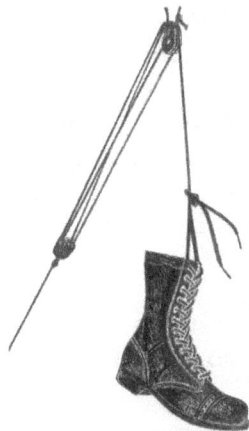

the boys. They were intensely curious about what I was doing, but they knew not to speak unless spoken to.

Next, I took a ball stretcher, a leather cuff designed to buckle around the loose skin of the scrotum above the testicles. I secured one on Kevin's balls and another on Bob's. I also gave their straining hard cocks a few strokes just for good measure, and my own entertainment.

The ball stretchers I was using were made for me by a friend who does leatherwork. They included a couple of leather straps that descended along the front and back of the testicles and ended in steel "D" rings. These were securely sewn and capable of holding significant weight.

As I finished putting the ball stretcher on Bob, I bent lower and began to untie his military boots. He glanced nervously down. I had told him to wear an old pair of boots, but knowing Bob, that meant he would spend an hour or two giving them a military quality spit shine.

"Nice shine you got on your boots, Pig," I said as I untied the second boot. "Now lift your foot."

Bob complied and barked another, "Sir, yes Sir" as he did. Damn I liked playing with these guys, that crisp edge they had really made the scene more fun for me.

I tossed the pair of boots into the space between them, then walked over to Kevin and did the same. I saw them looking at each other with puzzled looks as I tossed Kevin's boots next to Bob's.

"Those boots sure look good, pigs," I said with a hint of sarcasm. "You sure they are old?"

Almost in unison the two men shouted, "Sir, yes Sir."

I smiled, "Good cause I wouldn't want to ruin a new pair."

I watched their eyes as their puzzled look turned to one of downright mystery.

I then took another piece of nylon rope and tied it to Bob's ball stretcher. Giving it a tug to make sure it was tight I saw Bob grimace a little. I also noticed his cock spring back to full erection. That is a pretty good indicator of whether or not a man is enjoying a scene, though as far as body language goes it is anything but subtle.

I ran the rope to the lower pulley of one of the block and tackles hanging from the branch. By doing this, any weight or force put on the pulley arrangement would exert quadruple the force on the rope attached to Bob's balls. Then I did the same to Kevin.

Leaning down, I picked up Kevin's boots and tied the laces together. "Wouldn't want these to get mixed up would we pigs?"

"Sir, No Sir." They said still a little confused.

I then tied the pair of boots by their laces to the rope leading from Kevin's block and tackle. First I pulled the rope down, taking up any slack and lifting Kevin's balls almost vertically from his body. He took a sharp breath.

"Do you feel that Pig Number 1?"

"Sir, yes Sir."

"Good," I barked back. Then I pulled a couple of plastic bags from my pocket and put them in the boots, the mouth of the bags at the opening of the boot. I folded the rim of the bags over the top of the boots forming a waterproof lining in each shoe.

Then I walked very close to Kevin, getting right in his face. I stared right into his eyes and spoke very slowly and distinctly.

"Now Pig number 1, we are going to play a little game."

"Sir, yes Sir," he said in a much more subdued voice.

"And like any game there are rules, do you understand?" I was speaking softly but with as much of a commanding presence as I could muster. Everything inside me just wanted to smile at the thought of these two handsome men tied up to trees willing to let me have my way with them. I managed to stifle any sign of a grin.

"Sir, yes Sir."

"Good, here are the rules," I said in almost a whisper. "As long as you are having a good time, you will address me as Sir. But if things get too intense for you, or you urgently need to speak, you will address me by my name, do you understand?"

"Sir, I understand Sir."

I smiled and ran my hand over his bristling hair. "Good, cause we are going to have a good time."

Stepping close to Bob I delivered the same instructions, making sure he understood the rules and how he could let me know that he needed to either stop or slow down. Then I tied his boots to the other block and tackle in the same way I did Kevin's.

By now we had a circle of men standing a respectful distance away watching. I looked up at the gathering crowd and motioned them forward a little. "You fellows might want to step in a little closer so you can get a good look at how I am going to train these two pigs."

I looked around at Kevin and Bob, both trying to hide the eagerness on their faces, and unable to hide their raging erections. "You two Pigs are pretty smart aren't you?"

"Sir, yes Sir." They said in unison, with a little hesitancy not quite knowing what I was up to.

"I hear you two even went to college before you went into the Marines, is that right pigs?"

"Sir, yes Sir."

"College educated pigs. Nice. And just where did you two get all that ed-u-kay-shun?" I said adding a little of my Texas accent back into my voice.

"Sir, Texas A & M, Sir," They said, a little out of cadence.

"Texas A & M?" I shouted with a hint of irony in my voice. The crown chuckled, suspecting where I was going with this line of questions.

"That would make you two a couple of Aggies, wouldn't it?"

"Sir, yes Sir"

Aggie was the nickname given to alumni of A&M, referring to the agricultural roots of the university. Aggie was both a name used with pride by alumni and used as a derisive term by other universities. The Aggie joke had become a whole genre of humor much like the "dumb blond" jokes were. That was what I intended to use to spice this scene up a little.

"Well I understand that Aggies may have themselves a diploma and lots of "book learning", but most of the times they can't even pour piss out of a boot, even with the instructions written on the heels."

"Sir, no Sir."

The crowd laughed at the exchange and a few of them began to suspect what was about to happen.

"Well I don't know if I believe that, pigs. So I guess we are going to have to find out."

Bob looked at Kevin with a look of bewilderment but Kevin just broke into a slight smile and choked back a chuckle.

"Of course that means we need some boots full of piss to test this theory, isn't that right pigs?"

"Sir, I guess so Sir," Kevin said choking back a laugh.

"You guess so, pig?" I said, turning on my heels and confronting him just inches from his face. "You guess so? If I said it, it IS SO, do you understand, pig?"

Just to make my point I tugged down on the pair of boots hanging from his block and tackle. He winced and shouted.

"Sir yes Sir, whatever you say Sir!"

That action got a big laugh from the crowd. That also really worked for me. Sometimes I enjoy playing in front of a group, not just to feel my ego, but because the group energy makes the scene more fun.

"That's better," I said and walked to a friend who was watching sipping on a bottle of water.

"You think you could help these boys out with this little experiment?"

My friend got the idea immediately and nodded, "with pleasure."

He walked over to the pair of boots hanging from Kevin's pulley and gently tugged them down; they hung just about waist level. After testing them, he unzipped his jeans and pulled out his formidable cock. Pulling the boot close to it, he watched Kevin's face as he let a stream of steaming piss start flowing into the boot. The actual weight of the liquid was not very much, but pulling the boot down to fill it made the block and tackle pull tightly on Kevin's ball stretcher.

The others in the group followed his lead and soon there was a line of guys waiting to add their piss to the boots. In a few minutes the boots were full and sloshing with urine, the added weight had both boys standing on tiptoe to try to ease the weight pulling on their balls.

"How does that feel, pig number 2?" I stepped closer to Bob and he grimaced.

"Sir, heavy Sir."

"Honest answer, pig. Good for you."

Looking at the men tied to the trees, their balls distended from their bodies by the ropes and their firm cocks bobbing in the sunshine was a real turn-on for myself and the other men present. Sometimes there is nothing better than playing outside.

Once the boots were full and sloshing, the two marines were twisting against the belts in agony. Well, they really weren't in too much pain, even with the block and tackles the weight exerted on their balls was only about 12 pounds, and most of that was distributed to the skin of their scrotum and abdomen. Most of their writhing was caused not only by the weight, but all the hot men pissing in their boots, and them not being able to touch them.

When I decided they had about enough of the game, I took he belts from around them and freed them from the trees, but not before I used a couple of pairs of handcuffs to secure their wrists behind their backs. Now they were able to move around a bit, but still were strung up by the balls to the piss filled boots.

"So I guess you Aggies want to show everyone that you can pour piss from a boot, don't you?" I laughed as I pulled out a cigar and lit it.

The two men were panting and slightly confused. "Sir, how would you like us to do that, Sir?" asked Kevin.

"Be creative pigs. Show us how smart Aggies really are."

"Sir, yes Sir."

And with that they began working their way out of the predicament I had them in. Both figured they would back up to the boots and grab them, but because they couldn't see they only managed to bump into the hanging boots and slosh piss on one another. (Another benefit of playing outdoors is that you can get messy without any worries, cleanup is as simple as a garden hose.)

Finally Bob managed to grab a boot, but by them he was laughing so much he fumbled it and poured the contents on Kevin's back. Kevin shrieked and tried to butt Bob, but only succeeded in making the pulley jerk his balls tighter. Finally he did manage to empty the boot and I called a halt to the game.

"Good for you, pigs. Looks like Aggies can pour piss from a boot after all!" I took out a pocketknife and sliced through the ropes attached to their ball stretchers and the boots fell to the ground with a splash in a puddle of piss. By this time, both men as well as the group gathered to watch were laughing. Once I released Kevin and Bob's hands from the handcuffs, the hugged me gratefully and I removed the ball stretchers.

Afterward, I hosed them both down and sent them off to change into clean clothes for the club cookout that night. The next week, a box of very nice cigars arrived at my house with a thank you note from two grateful men long with an invitation to their commitment ceremony in a couple of weeks. Ain't love wonderful?

Hot Stuff

Sometimes those lessons you learned in college really come in handy. For me it was the biology courses I remembered. All that time dissecting dead critters, and what I got from it was a good idea for the tools of the trade. We used to use a variety of instruments, but one, the "teasing needle" a simple probe really, gave me an idea. I filed it away and years later finally had a chance to use it.

I had known Mistress for many years, and we had had quite a few adventures together over that time. She lived out of town now and we only got together occasionally these days so her visit was something special. She had planned to stay a few days for a series of workshops at a leather event in town and knowing Mistress, she would have at least one or two boys lined up for her amusement.

I met her at the airport, her face beamed as she saw me waiting at the baggage claim. After hugging like a couple of long lost siblings, I helped her get her luggage from the carrousel. Three suitcases, one of which was filled with toys and the other two with fetish ware and an extensive wardrobe for the three days she would be in town. Three suitcases was light for Mistress.

Once we got to my truck, and I had her luggage loaded safely in the back, I hoped in the cab with her and took off to the hotel where the event was taking place.

"So I was wondering if you had your dance card full for the weekend?" I asked with a provocative edge to my voice.

"Well, that depends on what you mean by full." She said with a wink. "I do have a couple of boys lined up that are just desperate for a good beating from me, and one of them was hinting about something more intimate."

"Any chance that would include CBT?" I asked, now sounding more than slightly interested.

"There just might be some of that indeed. Now what on earth could you be thinking to ask me such a question?" She fluttered her eyes in a passable impersonation of a Southern Belle.

"Well, you know, I do have some experience with that kind of thing and thought that if you'd like, I could help out."

Mistress chuckled and then purred, "I was kind of hoping you might be interested. You know I love watching you work, and especially if the boy you are working on ends up very grateful to me, for letting you play with him."

"I suspect he might be afterward." I replied. I knew Mistress had a stable of men who she called her "boys" who would go through anything to please her. Later they would be rewarded by something more intimate, and I would not be part of that, but that was OK.

"What nasty tricks did you have in mind?" Mistress crossed her legs and turned in the cab to face me.

"Well let's just say I have an experiment I'd like to try."

She shifted in her seat. "Now you've done it. You've gone and made me all hot and bothered. I know how much fun your experiments can be."

We continued our banter all the way to the hotel. Once I got her safely into the lobby and called a bellhop, I left her to register and gave her my room number so we could get together and plan the festivities later.

We arranged to meet up at a party being thrown by one of the local business owners at their house. The place was not palatial, but very comfortable and graced with a beautiful back yard complete with a large pool. Most importantly, they had high privacy fences and understanding neighbors. Later I found they too were kinky!

I arrived at the party about an hour after it started. I brought with me a small case containing just the materials I would need for the scene with Mistress' boys and not much else. I rarely travel with a full compliment of toys, since they can be not only heavy but cumbersome. No reason to bring everything including the kitchen sink.

I asked our hosts if Mistress had arrived and hey pointed me to the backyard. After getting a glass of mineral water, I walked outside and found a variety of scenes going on. Most were engaged in bondage or other quiet scenes, since they wanted to respect the neighbors. A few folks had decided to relax in the pool and since there were privacy fences, they had shed their party clothes for a warm evening skinny dip.

One of the great things about the leather/fetish community is their acceptance of all shapes and body types as well as all sexual orientations. There were lesbian couples swimming and playing together, gay male couples relaxing and smoking cigars and mixed sex groupings of every possible combination. The term pansexual has become popular to refer to these kinds of gatherings and I have to say that, though I am a gay man, I really enjoy them.

I found Mistress relaxing in a lawn chair with her two boys, actually men about 30, kneeling at her side. One was holding a plate of hors d'oeuvres and the other her drink.

As I approached she spoke to one boy, "Get Sir a chair, he will be joining us."

The obedient boy handed his counterpart the drink he was holding and sprinted to the other side of the patio to fetch a chair for me. Before I could even finish setting my toy bag down he returned with another lawn chair.

"Sir, if you wish to sit?" he asked in his best polite fashion.

I smiled and nodded. Sitting beside Mistress I took her hand and kissed it gently in a sign of affection and a show of mock chivalry. After all, we both are from the South.

"I see you brought your tools with you?" she smiled at me with a twinkle in her eye.

"I always carry a few little things. You never know when the opportunity may arise to play with a willing subject." I grinned back at her and noticed the boys now kneeling at her side again. They looked a little nervous.

"What did you bring?" She looked at the bag with genuine curiosity.

I opened the bag and pulled out a small leather case, inside were 8 small instruments. They were teasing needles from a dissecting kit. The needles are nothing more than a small wooden dowel with a 5 inch pointed probe attached. They are inexpensive and not very sharp, but still they raised the eyebrows of the two boys.

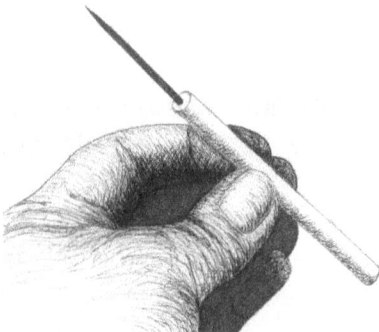

I handed the case to Mistress and she examined them with interest.

"Just what do you do with these? Surely you don't pierce the skin, they aren't sterile."

"I would never use a non-sterile needle to pierce the skin, you know me better than that." I said with a hint of sarcasm in my voice. As she examined the needles I opened he wrapper of a cigar and bit the end off.

One of the boys lunged forward with a cigarette lighter.

"My goodness, you do have them trained well, don't you, Mistress," I said, waving the boy off. "But I prefer a hotter flame for lighting my cigars."

I reached into the toy bag an pulled out a butane torch with an automatic igniter. I squeezed the trigger and the torch burst into a bright blue flame. This not only surprised the boys but caused them to shrink back slightly behind Mistress' chair. I lit my cigar with the noisy blue flame and after taking a few puffs, extinguished the torch.

I smiled at Mistress and said between puffs. "Bet you didn't think I had one that big, did you?"

She chuckled and extended a hand. "That is a very nice gadget you have there, where did you get that?"

I handed her the torch and replied, "Local hardware store of course."

Our town is blessed with a really extensive hardware store nestled in the gay district of the city. The store is an old fashioned hardware store with knowledgeable salespeople and everything imaginable, including an array of tack for horses as well as pet supplies including dog collars and more. Needless to say, the kinky crowd patronizes the place searching for "pervertibles", normal items that can be used for our kinky games.

"As I said, I would never use a non-sterilized needle to pierce the skin."

At that the boys again gave each other quizzical looks.

"I use them only when they are red hot, and I have found there is no need to do more than simply touch the surface of the skin to get the desired effect."

Mistress was obviously interested and handed the torch back to me. "So I guess you are going to have to show me how this all works."

"I'd be delighted, if I had a willing volunteer." I looked at the two boys who nervously turned their eyes away.

Mistress leaned toward them. "So which of your two would like to play with Sir tonight? And this is not an order, it is a genuine question that I expect an honest answer to."

After a bit of hesitation the taller blond man leaned over to her and whispered in her ear.

She smiled and glance in my direction, then whispered something in reply.

Turning to me she said, "Seems like this nice boy here is interested. He's read your book and really wants to experience some of your ideas first hand."

I chuckled and nodded, "Glad to hear it. I suspect he might even enjoy the sensations, especially if they are done to him while he is in your arms."

Mistress positively beamed. She leaned over to the boy and gave him instructions. In seconds he was naked and standing at her side.

"Now, boy," she said standing up and walking behind him, "I want you to lean back against me, not too hard, but just enough so I can support you."

He did as she requested and she wrapped her arms around his chest.

"Hands behind your head, boy," she commanded.

He obeyed without hesitation. Then she motioned to the other boy to stand behind her and steady her. He did, making a Mistress sandwich, and making her smile. Once she was secure, I pulled up the chair facing the boy's crotch. I ran my hands along his flat abdomen and felt the ripples of his well-toned muscles. Mistress always seemed to have a never-ending supply of hot bodies around her!

I moved lower to the well trimmed patch of blond pubic hair and his slowly hardening cock. Taking it in my hand I stroked it a couple of times and looked up at him.

"This might get in the way." I said as I whipped out a large pocket knife.

He jumped with alarm, and Mistress let out an intake of breath followed by a hearty chuckle. Meanwhile, I reached into my toy bag and pulled out a hank of rope. I used the knife to cut off a piece about 6 feet long and then dropped the hank and the knife back into the bag.

I tied a loop of rope around the head of his now rigid penis and stood up. Moving close to his face I whispered, "Open your mouth boy."

He did as requested and I placed the other end of the rope in his teeth. He bit down, knowing that was going to be my next order.

"See what a clever boy he is?" Mistress said, restraining another chuckle.

The rope pulled his cock up flat against his belly, leaving his balls exposed and available for my fun.

Next I pulled out the torch. I clicked the igniter and it spewed forth a hot blue flame. I pointed it away from myself and the boy and held the tip of one of the teasing needles in the flame. Soon it glowed bright red. Then I turned to face the boy's contracting testicles.

"Don't move a muscle, boy," I said as I brought the red hot tip near the skin of his balls. Quickly, without piercing the skin, I touched the hot needle to his skin, not too much pressure, and removed it after it made a small hiss.

He twitched involuntarily and Mistress held him tighter. She could feel him writhing against her body as the endorphins began rushing through him.

I heated another needle and did the same thing to the other side of his balls. Again he twitched and this time he let out a moan that gave me shivers. I love hearing people moan when I play with them. It lets me know something I am doing is working. I really dislike stoic people who endure the pain with no expression or noise. For me moans and groans are the real music of the dungeon and the sounds really get me excited.

I took the needle and heated it again, touching another spot on his balls. This time he shuddered and whimpered, "Oh wow."

"Oh wow, indeed." I echoed. He was beginning to really get off on the feelings that the hot points were triggering in his body. By the fourth time I touched his flesh with the needles he was flying. I watched Mistress as she absorbed his energy, she was getting very aroused by the scene, and that is what I had hoped.

The body reacts to heat very quickly. It's a defense mechanism. It's what keeps us from holding our hand in a flame. The heat triggers an immediate response. Since the tiny burns the needles were inflicting were so small, they would heal almost immediately, but to the body's defense system they were still burns and that caused a cascade of pain numbing chemicals to start flowing. That's why he was reacting the way he was. He was getting high from the overload of endorphins and other natural opiates the body was producing. Similar to a "runner's high," this feeling causes a mild euphoria that was enhanced by the sexual nature of the scene.

After a few more delicate touches of the red-hot needles, I could tell he was "done". He was writhing against Mistress and having a great time, but I didn't want him to be incoherent. Mistress had other plans for him later and he would need energy for that.

Behind Mistress, the other boy acing as her support was enjoying the scene, too. Mistress pressing into him and the shared feelings of the scene had him going as well. I could see, even though his eyes were closed, he was writhing as well. Mistress was smiling and happy and so was I.

I turned off the torch and stood in front of the boy. Wrapping my arms around him and Mistress I gave him a long hug. I pulled the rope from his teeth and gave him a lingering kiss before stepping away and untying the rope from his still rigid penis.

"You are going to thank Sir properly, aren't you, boy?" Mistress purred in his ear.

At that the boy dropped to his knees and began kissing my boots. Mistress certainly knew how to train her boys.

Remote Control

I usually find lots of devices in hardware stores that can be easily perverted to kinky purposes, but sometimes I find "pervertables" in surprising spots. I was at the local pet store buying kitty litter and decided to stroll down the pet-toy aisle. Our cats are surrogate children for my boy and I, so occasionally we buy them toys. Fortunately we learned that there is a rule for cat toys. The more expensive the toy, the less likely the cat will have any interest in it. I found this out by splurging on a very expensive battery powered toy once, that our cats completely ignored. They did however get hours of enjoyment from the box it came in. Lesson learned.

As I walked past the dog collars, a glass case caught my eye. Inside was a very nice looking equipment case; the kind made of molded plastic with a foam interior. Inside was what looked like a nylon webbing dog collar and a small keychain sized remote control. The device was actually a training collar for dogs that consisted of a nylon collar with a small receiver attached. Protruding from the receiver were two pointed metal posts. They didn't seem sharp enough to pierce the skin, but with a sufficient point to work their way through the dog's coat and touch the skin. My interest very piqued, I got a salesperson to open the case.

They were horrified that I wanted to see the device they considered just short of inhumane. It seems that this collar could deliver a mild electric shock to the animal at the discretion of the owner whenever they made too much

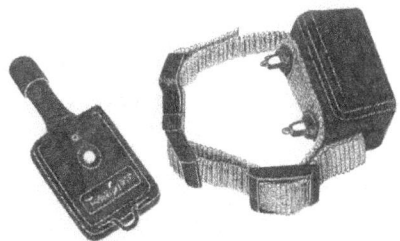

noise or misbehaved. The shock, according to the literature that came with the collar, was perfectly safe and would only serve to get the dog's attention.

Immediately, I did a little calculation. If it was safe for a 25 pound poodle, it would certainly be safe enough for a 155 pound boy. (When I use the term boy, I am referring to an adult male or sometimes female who identifies as a boy. I have absolutely no interest in anyone who might be under the age of 21, and mostly not under the age of 35.)

Though this gadget was pricey, about $125, I quickly decided I must have it, and I whipped out my plastic for a quick purchase. The clerks continued to stare daggers through me as I walked from the store with a bag of cat food and an electric shock collar. I feel pretty sure they thought I was intending to use the gadget to train my cat! Of course I didn't explain, besides sometimes it's nice to have people be a little afraid of you.

Once I got home I opened my new toy, after feeding the cats, and put the batteries in both the collar and the remote control. The collar was pretty big, So I measured one of my leather cock rings and cut the nylon strap down to a more appropriate size. I figured this would be just right to fit under a boy's scrotum, and his natural body moisture would serve as a good electrolyte to assure good contact. Sweat contains a lot of salts and they are critical for good conduction.

Once I had used a cigar lighter to melt the frayed end of the strap, a good idea to prevent it from unraveling, I was ready for a trial run. Since I don't like to do anything to someone else without having at least some idea of what it does, I dropped my pants and strapped the collar on my own cock and balls. The small box containing the receiver fit snuggly under my scrotum and was not in the least uncomfortable. The metal points were almost undetectable pressing against my balls. Not bad so far.

Next I found the remote and examined it closely. There were three settings, "L", "M" and "H". It didn't take a genius to know what these meant. I chose "M" and after setting the control, I sat down before pushing the button. Good thing I did, the jolt might have made me loose my footing. I wasn't expecting it to be so sharp. It would definitely get a boy's attention!

I tried it again, and now that I knew what to expect, it wasn't so bad. Just for grins I tried the high setting. That was more intense, but nothing outrageous. This would be a GOOD TOY!

I removed the collar and used alcohol to wipe down the points. Though there was no body fluid on them, I always like to keep my toys clean. I then put the toy back into its case and packed it away in my toy bag for future use.

A couple of months later I was attending a conference of leatherfolk in Chicago and thought it would be a good time to try out my new toy. The conference was taking place at one of the largest hotels in the city, and that weekend the mezzanine bar in the lobby was packed with leathermen and women. There were lots of willing boys who wanted to play and after negotiation with one particularly eager man, I gave him the collar and told him how to put it on. Then I told him we had only a few minutes before the courtesy bus for one of the local leather bars was leaving from the hotel, so we would play a little at the bar.

He had a puzzled look on his face as he went off to his room to change for the evening out. I fingered the remote hanging from my key chain and began imagining the fun I was going to have later in the evening.

He returned all decked out in his best "boy wear", slightly worn jeans, leather vest and a leather ball cap. He fell into step behind me and we headed off for the shuttle. The bar was across town and was one of the legendary leather bars of Chicago. Though it was small, it made up for its diminutive size by the sheer number of leathermen present. Like the hotel lobby bar, it was packed.

After getting my bearings, I found a few friendly faces I knew from back in Texas. We chatted for a while and the boy stood attentively at my side. Soon I got thirsty and I handed him a $20 and told him to go get my friends and me a drink. He took our orders and was headed off eager as a puppy when I stopped him.

"Now, I want you to bring back those drinks, but don't you dare spill a drop."

He nodded and sprinted off, apparently he had forgotten the device attached to his balls. I watched him from the corner of my eye and told my friends to watch closely. I then showed them the remote control and they smiled with the delight only Sadists (and I mean that in a good way) can have. As I saw him with his hands full of plastic glasses turn away from the bar, I pushed the button on the remote control.

At once I heard a loud scream, and he fumbled one of the glasses, spilling it down his pants. The sound was much too loud to have come from just him, and when I looked around I saw at least three other boys clutching their crotches! It only took me a moment to realize that a few other Daddies, Tops and otherwise kinky folk had been shopping at the pet stores. The collars apparently all had the same frequency.

After a round of laughter that spread through the bar like a wave, I saw a few other men pull out their keys. One of them caught my eye and smiled a sadistic grin. As he pressed the button, shouts erupted from various locations in the bar. More drinks were spilled and soon boys were dancing and holding their crotches like Michael Jackson!

I made the rounds and found the other guys that had similar remotes and we compared ideas. Before the evening was over, we had worn out the boys and our batteries.

The Mummy Rises

CBT is usually part of a bigger picture for me. I love to use it as part of a scene, but rarely as the entire scene. Since most of my friends and acquaintances know my enthusiasm for CBT, they often ask me to participate with them in those that may involve CBT as part of the whole scene. Sometimes being known as a specialist has its benefits, especially when it comes to getting to play with a wide variety of people!

I was one of the founders of a public playspace here in my hometown of Dallas. Though it no longer exists, the Inquisition was a great spot with a lot of really positive energy. It was little more than a warehouse outfitted with every imaginable piece of dungeon gear and a small social area. Though pretty basic, it provided a place where local as well as players from across the country could really let loose without fear of shocking the newcomers. This led to a lot of very fun parties and often some legendary scenes.

I had a couple of friends from out of town who had come to one of our weekend parties and asked me to help out with a scene. The couple, both men in their mid 40's, were always fun to be with and I had played with each of them individually before, but never together. The scene they planned promised to be fun.

The main event was mummification. If you are not familiar with this scene, let me give you a brief description. Like the famed Egyptian mummies, a mummification scene has some similarities. The most striking difference is that the subject to be wrapped is alive and will be very much alive after the scene as well. We started by having our subject, Roy strip. That part I always enjoy, I guess I just like seeing naked men, go figure.

Since he was going to be getting warm during the scene, we put folded hand towels under his arms and between his legs to absorb any sweat. Then we used a large roll of plastic wrap for the first layer of the mummy. While Roy was still standing, we began wrapping the plastic around his body. Starting at the waist, to secure his hands, we wrapped several times around him moving slowly upward so each successive wrap overlapped the one below. Once we reached his shoulders, we turned the roll to go across the right shoulder and over the chest. The next wrap moved up his back, over his left shoulder and over his chest.

Roy turned his body to assist in the wrapping. We left his legs and feet until last so he could retain his balance and help out with the plastic wrap layer. His partner Jim and I were both watching Roy carefully to make sure he didn't fall over while doing this first layer. The plastic wrap was secure around Roy, but not too tight. We wanted to make sure he could still breathe without any restriction of his chest.

Once we were done with the chest and shoulders, we cut the plastic and began a new wrap around his legs. For this, Roy remained still and Jim and I did all the work. We wrapped his legs with plastic in the same way as his upper body, finishing just above the feet.

Now it was time to move Roy to a table. Nearby there was a nice padded massage table positioned just for the scene. Jim and I tipped Roy backward into Jim's arms and I took his feet. We lifted him up and positioned him on the table on his back before continuing.

Once he was in position, we finished off his feet with a few layers and then moved to his head. Jim carefully wrapped the plastic over Roy's face, leaving his nose and mouth uncovered. Plastic soon covered his chin and neck, carefully positioned to not constrict his throat, but still covering every square inch with wrap. I took a bandage scissors and cut a thin strip of plastic that went over his upper lip just below his nose. Now only his lips and nostrils were exposed.

Some people do a mummification with just plastic wrap. The feeling for the bottom is very secure, immobile and tight. However since the wrap is so thin and light, a lot of sensations still get through. For this scene, Roy wanted a lot more sensory deprivation than just plastic wrap would provide. That's where the duct tape comes in.

Using strips of duct tape, I began carefully covering Roy's body. I started at the shoulders and layered strips in a diagonal pattern, slightly overlapping each strip. The effect made a herringbone pattern as the strips from first the right shoulder and then the left shoulder were overlapped and woven together. I continued down Roy's body with the duct tape until he was covered from neck to toes in the smooth gray tape.

Now, with the help of a couple of friends who were attending the party, we carefully rolled Roy face down on the table. Again we used duct tape to create the herringbone pattern and cover his back. Jim checked in with Roy occasionally to be sure he was doing well and enjoying the scene.

Sometimes scenes with this much restriction and sensory deprivation cause the bottom to panic. That's why we kept a couple of pairs of round edge bandage scissors nearby at all times.

Once Roy was fully wrapped in tape, we flipped him over again and began covering his head and face. We carefully wrapped tape strips over his nose, leaving the nostrils exposed and over his mouth, leaving his lips exposed for breathing and communication.

Additionally, if Roy was going to stay in the mummy for any period of time, he might need a sip of water to avoid dehydration. We had a water bottle and straw on hand as well.

When Roy was fully encased in the mummy, Jim took a folded T-shirt and put it under Roy's head as a pillow. Now we took a break, and I went to get both Jim and me a couple of bottles of soda. I had worked up a sweat. Making mummies is hard work.

For most people, being mummified is a very enjoyable scene. Reports of having "out of body" experiences are numerous and the "floating" sensation that comes from the sensory deprivation is almost universal. I have always found it best to have a quiet place for a mummification to keep the bottom calm and let them experience fully the process and sensory fun.

Jim and I took turns watching over Roy, in case he needed something or wanted to get out of the mummy. Panic is rare for people who enjoy extreme bondage, but just in case, I always keep bandage scissors handy to get them out fast if need be.

After about a half an hour, I could see that Roy was breathing very calmly and seemed to be drifting well into his scene. At about 45 minutes, Jim and I used our fingers to lightly stroke the sides of Roy's body through the mummy casing. He shivered from our touch; the absence of sensation for so long makes any touch amplified.

That is exactly the response I wanted. Roy was now sensory deprived, but highly aware, and that meant anything we did to him would be multiplied by the tricks his mind would play on him.

I carefully snipped a small incision in the mummy casing right between Roy's legs. Just below his crotch. Moving upward with one finger inserted through the slit in the tape and plastic, I slowly cut a small opening just around his cock and balls. Roy shivered again as the cool air of the dungeon caressed his genitals. His cock begin growing almost immediately, a good sign.

I let his skin adjust to the air and watched his cock harden. Jim took it in his hand and stroked it a few times, making Roy moan like a mummy from a "B" horror movie. Holding back a laugh, I opened my toy bag and pulled out a few special things I had brought.

First was a green abrasive sponge, he plastic kind used for scrubbing sinks. It was a brand new one, and had never had detergent on it. Using an old one would risk an allergic reaction to any chemicals in the detergent. I took the cleaning pad and held it in my palm, then slowly and deliberately wrapped it around the shaft of his cock. As I gently squeezed it he moaned again and wriggled uncomfortably. I released my grip and then tightened it again, causing a similar sensation.

Sensations like the one caused by the scouring pad are not very impressive if you see what is causing them, but if you have been drifting without stimulation for 45 minutes it makes a big difference.

I removed the pad after a few more squeezes and Jim stroked Roy's cock again. It sprang back to full attention as he did. His moans changed back to pure pleasure. Now I brought out a small wire cleaning brush. It looked like a toothbrush but made of brass wires. I carefully touched the brush to the underside of Roy's balls. He jumped like he had been shocked with electricity! The prickly metal bristles must have felt like needles on his sensitive balls. Every time I touched them, his cock jumped and his whole body thrashed inside the duct tape cocoon.

Next I let Jim stroke him a little more. His cock was stretched and rigid, the head of his penis almost purple it was so engorged with blood. I took advantage of that for my next sensation. I had a garden glove in my toy box. This was the kind studded with hundreds of little rubber dots to help you grip things that might otherwise slip through your fingers.

I donned the glove and slowly wrapped my hand around the throbbing head of Roy's cock. As I slowly twisted my fist around the head, the little rubber spots caused friction with the skin of his dick. The sensation must have been very intense because Roy tried to scream through the tiny opening in the mummy for his lips. I stopped, holding his cock in my grip but not moving for a moment until he calmed down. Then, I once again twisted my grip and Roy bucked up off the table a little ways before mumbling another scream.

We continued with this torture for a while longer and then I let him rest. Jim returned to stroking his cock as I watched. We were alternating between pleasurable sensations and painful ones, and though the actual torture was very mild, to Roy it was intense.

I now pulled out a favorite toy of mine. It is a vibrating urethral sound. A sound is a medical device used to clear adhesions and obstructions in the urethra. This one was a stainless steel rod attached to a stainless steel battery compartment. The medical use for this device is questionable. Supposedly it emits ultrasonic waves that help to unblock an obstruction in the urethra, but after asking several urologists they said it was not used much and was of questionable value.

As a sex toy it has great value! The vibrations are very high frequency and they are a real delight when applied to the penis or scrotum. I did not use the sound inside the urethra since it was not sterile, however if properly sterilized it can have an interesting effect when inserted. Personally, I find it more stimulating outside the penis than inside. More nerve endings on the outside, therefore, more fun!

I touched the vibrating rod against the base of his penis just above the balls and saw him react. At first there was a sharp jerk as though he had been shocked, but soon he realized is was just a vibration and he relaxed. Some.

I slowly moved the vibrating rod over his tight scrotum and teased him underneath his balls. Then moved it back to the shaft of the penis and slowly moved up to the head. His cock twitched and jumped as the vibrating sound moved over his skin. He began to moan and his cock twitched over and over. Before he become too aroused, I pulled the vibrator away.

I waited a few moments and watched the twitching in his penis subside. Then I started again, moving the vibrating sound on a different pattern over his balls and up his cock. Again his dick began jumping and visibly throbbing. I stopped again, letting him relax a little.

I continued this several more times until his body gave signs that he could no longer restrain himself. I motioned to Jim, who had already coated his hand with lube and was ready to take over. He took hold of Roy's cock, still throbbing from the vibrator and gave it a few long strokes, the slick lube letting his big hand slide smoothly over the skin of Roy's penis. Suddenly, Roy's body arched from the table and he stiffened. His cock erupted in a volcano of cum and he let out a shrill whimper through the mouth slit of the mummy wrapping. Jim continued to stroke his spasming penis and drained every bit of cum from him before stopping.

Once Roy had finally calmed down, I took a couple of paper towels and handed them to Jim. He carefully and tenderly cleaned the cum from Roy's still hard cock, then placed his hands on Roy's chest and felt his breathing as it returned to normal. Jim leaned over and hugged the mummified body of Roy, feeling the heat and energy he was still radiating from his orgasm.

After they had shared the moment, I pulled out my bandage scissors and began slitting the mummy-casing open, starting at the feet. I slowly cut the wrapping all the way to his crotch, then continued above the crotch to his neck. I cut across the shoulder and up the side of Roy's head, carefully avoiding scratching his skin. Then Jim and I pulled the casing apart at the cut and exposed Roy's body to the air of the dungeon. I could almost see heat ripples rise from his body.

Inside the mummy, the temperature can rise to quite toasty levels, and since now Roy's body was being exposed to the cool room temperature of the Dungeon, he began to shiver a little. I pulled a couple of bath towels out of a sack that Jim had brought and laid them over Roy to warm him back up.

A few minutes later, he was dressed and ambulatory again. In the social area, we all discussed the scene and Roy and Jim thanked me for my assistance. I thanked them as well for a chance to be part of such an intense experience for Roy. Over a cup of coffee, he gave me a run down of what he thought we had done to him. His description was far more imaginative than anything I could have actually done. The mind, when set free of too much stimulation, fills in the details in imaginative ways.

Water Torture

Combining and experimenting with CBT techniques is what makes them so much fun for me. Sometimes it is a combination that happens from careful planning and sometimes it just happens in a flash of twisted insight. That is what happened one evening while I was visiting a friend's house for a small get together.

I had bought a small paddle that I thought would have been great for smacking a nice set of balls, and on a hunch I modified it with a series of notches down each side. The notches were not for any percussion effect, they were to make the paddle useful for cock and ball bondage as well as paddling.

I found a friend at the party who agreed to help me try out my new toy and once we found a clear space to play we began. Since this was a casual scene, intended more as an experiment than anything, we didn't go through any formal negotiations. He just undressed and hopped up on a makeshift table our hosts had set up in one of their spare rooms.

My friend, Bryan, loved CBT as much as me and he had both bottomed and Topped in scenes. We almost never used any protocol in our play since we knew each other so well and since we were both Tops. To anyone looking we must have seemed like a couple of kids playing with a new toy, and so we were.

I positioned the wide end of the paddle beneath his scrotum and let his cock lay along the length. I pulled a length of woven nylon rope from my toy bag and found the center of the piece. Threading the rope under the paddle and out through the first two notches, I looped the free ends around his cock and balls and drew them reasonably tight. I made sure I didn't pinch any skin between the ropes where they crossed. I wanted any pain I inflicted to be intentional.

The effect of the tightening loop was immediate. His cock began to swell just like it had a cock ring on it. I tied a simple knot in the rope and then pulled the ends down through the next two notches. Looping them up through the third set of notches, I criss-crossed the rope across his hardening cock and bound it to the paddle. I continued in this fashion up the length of the paddle, securing his hard cock to the wooden surface.

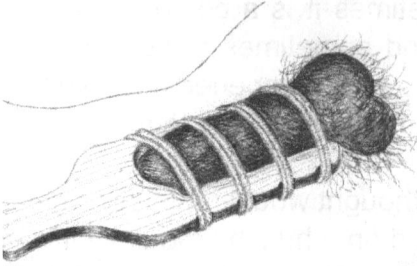

Once I got to the end, I wrapped another loop of rope around the head of his penis, just under the glans. This allowed me to secure the head tightly to the paddle as well. I then tied the rope beneath the paddle and took a moment to admire my handiwork.

Bryan looked down and smiled. "Looks pretty neat!"

"Nice and tidy." I nodded.

"That's a great idea for a small paddle." He complimented me.

"Yea," I agreed, "Seems kind of a waste to just let that cock go unused since it is all tied up nice and pretty."

Bryan gave me a suspicious look and then lay back on the table. "And just what did you have in mind?"

"Not sure, but I suspect it will work better with your hands and feet secure."

With that I pulled some more ropes from my bag and quickly had his hands and feet secured to the board with simple but effective ties.

"Why do I get the feeling you are going to do something that is going to be more intense than I expected?" Bryan asked with a slight smile.

By this time a couple of other men attending the party had wandered in to the room and in a spirit of camaraderie and mischievousness they began to conspire with me. One of the men was holding a bottle of water. I asked him if I could borrow it and he agreed with a raised eyebrow.

There was a hook in the ceiling above the table. I suspect it was for some kinky games our hosts played in private, but I didn't ask. I just reached up and hooked a finger into it and tested its strength. It seemed pretty strong, at least strong enough for a bottle of water.

I used another piece of rope to loop over the hook. Using some borrowed duct tape, I fastened the bottle, neck facing upward, to the rope. It hung conveniently directly over Bryan's cock. At least it did after we repositioned him a little. That is part of the fun of having co-conspirators in a scene, they can provide muscle when adjustments need to be made.

I then took a knife from my bag. When Bryan saw it he stiffened. "We didn't negotiate any knives!"

"No need to negotiate." I gave him an evil look and approached with the knife. After brandishing it in front of him, I took it and stabbed the bottom of the plastic bottle. "It's not for you."

He laughed nervously and relaxed a little. About that time the first drop of water fell from the bottle onto the vinyl covered table. By adjusting the cap on the bottle. Opening it slightly or closing it, I could adjust the speed of the drops. I fiddled with it a bit until the dripping was only once every few seconds.

I motioned my friends over to help reposition Bryan again and put his bound cock directly below the dripping bottle. The drops fell right on the underside of the head of his penis, the most sensitive part.

"Oh shit!" Bryan groaned. "You are gonna let that drip, aren't you?"

"Who me?" I smiled and backed off a ways, taking a roll of paper towels and making a make-shift pad of a few of them, I slid them under Bryan to soak up any runoff. The other men stood back and smiled. Together with them, I waited and watched. The first few minutes the steady drip, drip, drip was no problem for Bryan. He jerked a little as the cold water hit him but little changed.

We waited in silence, occasionally moving around to watch the steady slow dripping water. Bryan closed his eyes and tried to "zone out". In that way he could avoid the annoying sensation of the dripping. It wasn't working. He would be still for a few moments and then jerk a little and get a pained expression on his face.

His cock was still hard, though not as stiff as when we began. Not surprising since this had to be a very annoying feeling. One of my friends who was watching leaned in close and whispered to Bryan. "Confess!"

Bryan laughed, but only a little. The annoyance factor of the dripping was quickly making this a real torture scene. Bryan was starting to sweat, and it had only been 10 minutes. Lucky for him the bottle wasn't full and it would soon run out of water.

He was writhing and moaning by the time the bottle dripped its last. His breathing slowed once the water torment stopped and he opened his eyes and looked up at me with a combination of pleading and annoyance.

"Damn that is really annoying!" He said with a forced grin.

One of our friends brought another bottle and handed it to me.

"Oh good! Fresh supplies!"

Bryan's face shriveled into a scowl. "Red!"

"Had enough?" I asked with mock innocence.

Bryan stared daggers through me as I began to release him from the bondage. I untied his hands and feet first, then as I approached his bound penis and balls, he sat up and blocked my hands.

"I'll take it from here," he said.

Once he had finished extricating himself from the paddle and rope, he handed it to me.

"I think next time, I would prefer you just use the paddle on me."

As the men around me laughed, I hugged Bryan and he whispered in my ear.

"Payback is hell."

Butterflies Are Free

A Note about Safety and Technique.

I include this scene because of the growing popularity of temporary piercing. It is not intended as a step by step guide to this kind of play, but rather a glimpse at how temporary piercing and CBT can work together to create an extraordinary scene. Having said this, I want to reinforce that I am not advocating anyone do this without getting personal instruction from someone experienced in piercing and the precautions and procedures necessary to minimize risks.

Any scene involving invasive activities such as piercing require a good knowledge of not only the activity, but the possible repercussions of the activity. Any time you break the skin, you open up a tiny door to the interior of the body. This door is all it takes for an infection. The human body is covered with lots of microorganisms and bacteria that are harmless to us as long as they are outside our bodies, but given a direct access to the body's interior and the bloodstream, they can be not only pesky, but dangerous.

More recently MSRA, or methicillin-resistant Staphylococcus aureus has become a concern. MRSA is a type of bacterium that is resistant to penicillin and some other antibiotics. The bacteria get into the body through cuts in the skin, causing infection that can be debilitating if not treated early and with the appropriate antibiotics. In very rare cases MRSA can be lethal.

To minimize the risk of unwanted infection, I use a number of measures. First and foremost, I use only sterile, single use disposable needles for piercing. These can be obtained from surgical supply houses or veterinary supply companies. I also use a "sharps container". These can be purchased at any drug store. They are hard plastic containers designed to resist the points of needles. When they are full, they are sealed and disposed of. Ask your drug store what specific regulations are in effect in your area about the disposal of infectious waste. You don't want any trash handlers getting an accidental piercing and possible infection from your carelessness!

Needles come in many different sizes, from very thin short needles for injecting insulin (not suitable for play piercing) to extremely large needles used in surgical procedures. I prefer needles between 22 and 25 gauge. These are long enough and stiff enough not to bend when you least expect it, and still thin enough to not to cause too much pain or damage the skin beyond a tiny hole.

The tip of the needle is cut at an angle creating a very efficient device for piercing the skin. In temporary piercing, the object is to create a hole that will heal, unlike the kind of piercing done when a piece of jewelry is going to be left behind. Because of this, you try not to remove any skin from the hole, merely push it out of the way.

Prior to the piercing, I like to have my bottom clean the skin of his genitals well with an anti-microbial soap and dry the area with a clean towel. I position the bottom on his back, on a comfortable surface. (Here is where owning an old medical table comes in handy!)

The cock and balls are then positioned through the Butterfly board and the halves of the board are tied together and around the bottom to keep them in position. To avoid the testes natural defense mechanism of retracting, I sometimes put my bottom in a cockring prior to the scene.

I then use Techni-Care on a sterile gauze sponge to clean the skin surface just prior to the piercing. I apply the cleanser using a circular motion from the center working outward. I then allow this to air dry while I am preparing the needles for the scene. The needles will need to be removed from the paper envelopes they come in and set out on a clean secure surface. I like to use a clean paper towel on a medical instrument tray, but a TV tray or other portable stand will work as well. Just keep everything close and clean. This stand should also have the sharps container on it for easy disposal of the needles.

Another hazard is an accidental stick. Use care to avoid pricking yourself with the needles before and especially after the scene. Because of this possibility, I strongly suggest not trying to put the needles back into the plastic sheaths before discarding them. That is what the sharps container is for! Recapping needles is no longer done in surgery or medical procedures because of this hazard.

As I work, I try to keep my gloved hands from coming into contact with anything other than the bottom's cleaned skin and the materials I have prepared for the piercing. This minimizes the risk of accidental contamination of any broken skin.

When piercing the scrotum, care must be taken to avoid the larger blood vessels or any irregularities on the surface of the scrotal sack. The needles are inserted in one smooth move through the skin and into the foamcore below for a butterfly. For other play piercings no backing is used, so care must be taken to allow enough breathing room so the tip of the needle doesn't scratch the surrounding skin.

For a butterfly, I angle the needles away from the scrotum to help keep the skin slightly taught and to avoid the possibility of the needles being pulled out. I try to work symmetrically, first placing a needle in one side then the other to balance the pressure and tension on the scrotal sack.

I try not to use more than a dozen or so needles on a new bottom. The sensations are very intense, add to that the fear factor and the potential for a bottom becoming over-stimulated are great. By working slowly and calmly, I minimize the bottom's fears, and allow them to adjust to each piercing sensation. The body's endorphin pump works overtime during a scene like this, so I like to get feedback from my play partner constantly. Keeping the line of communication open helps me to calm them and gives me important information on how they are responding to the scene.

I remove the needles in one continuous smooth movement. They go immediately into the sharps container. After all the needles are removed, I clean the area again with Techni-Care, or if I am in a particularly sinister mood, I use a combination of Techni-Care and alcohol. The sting is a little extra treat!

Most of the holes will not bleed. If they do, I swab them with an extra sterile alcohol swab after the bleeding has stopped. Usually it won't be more than a drop or two, and the blood coming out actually helps clean out the hole from any extraneous material that might have gotten in. I have never encountered any profuse bleeding, but I would have no qualms about seeking medical attention should that occur.

I tell the bottom to check the area when they go home or in the morning when they shower to be sure there is no additional bleeding. I also tell them to clean the area with an antibacterial soap the following morning just to be sure.

It is not uncommon for a bottom to feel slightly dizzy or high after a temporary piercing scene, so don't rush the aftercare. I try to give them plenty of time to come down and adjust to reality again. This can take from a few minutes to several hours depending on how they respond. After a scene at a play party with one friend, I found him still dingy a full two hours later, so I drove him home myself to make sure he would be safely tucked in for the evening.

Checking with him the following morning, I learned he was fine and grateful for the extra measure of aftercare.

I sometimes attend a very special gathering of experienced leathermen in the woods somewhere up north. These gatherings are a combination of week-long play party, family reunion and SM Rodeo. Let me explain. For many of us in the leather community, gatherings such as this are the way we catch up with old friends who we may not have seen in a while, so there is a lot of chatting, jokes and general socialization. Additionally, the whole place, which is a converted campground and resort becomes a private play zone for all kinds of BDSM activities and just plain sex.

Since it is just "us guys", nudity as well as hard core fetish wear is common. Being that it is a once a year event, some men like to make the occasion special by participating in scenes that some would describe as extreme or even edge-play. I cannot imagine a safer place to explore this kind of play, considering the skill level and number of experienced leathermen attending. Because of this, a lot of folks like to leave with souvenirs, marks that may take weeks to heal or at least fond memories of doing something that would be considered really scary back home.

It was at one of these gatherings that I saw my friend Ben doing a Butterfly Board on a willing bottom. I had heard about them many times and even seen a few pictures, but I had never watched it being done in person, and that made all the difference.

Ben was a slight man, some might even call him gentle looking. He is affable and easy to talk to, and it is that approachability that makes him even more intimidating as a Top. He just seems so innocent, and yet I knew his reputation and had seen him play before, so I knew he was what my circle calls a "monster player". His scenes were usually simple, but very intense and not for the squeamish.

It is by watching him perform the butterfly board that I learned to do it myself. Ben provided lots of tips and technique suggestions that I incorporated into my own play. For that I will be eternally grateful.

Ben was playing with another friend of mine who I had known for years. Gary was a good looking man in his mid-thirties who had a penchant for finding intense scenes. He liked to try new things and as a very experienced bottom, he was rarely panicked in a scene.

As Ben prepared him for the scene, I watched Gary and knew that this would be a very different experience for him. He had never done anything involving temporary piercing or any kind of invasive activity at all. He lay on a table set up in one of the several tents that the club had pitched for the event. To an outsider, the tents gave the place a look more like a circus lot than a gathering of leathermen.

Ben methodically laid out his tools. On a medical stand, he placed a box of needles. He took out a couple of dozen of the sterile single-use needles and arranged them on the stand. They were still in the plastic wrappers and capped. He then pulled out a bottle of skin cleanser and opened a fresh package of gauze pads.

Next, Ben donned a pair of surgical gloves with the skill of an operating room nurse. He took a few of the gauze pads and poured some of the disinfectant-cleanser on them. Then he began to gently scrub the skin of Gary's scrotum and penis with the pads.

Once he had finished he took a plastic bag from the table, inside it was a square of foam-core board. In the center of the board was a hole about 1.5 inches in diameter. He placed this board over Gary's penis and worked his testicles through the hole until his genitals were neatly positioned above the foam-core board. Next Ben wiped the board down with the same cleanser, blotting any excess with a fresh gauze pad.

Gary was trembling a little, and Ben gently laid his forearm on Gary's forehead. He spoke a few words of calming reassurance to Gary before proceeding. Once Gary had calmed, Ben took the first needle from the wrapper, he uncapped it and then held it in front of Gary's face. I watched Gary turn pale and begin trembling. Ben wanted Gary to see exactly what he was going to use on him. This both sent a rush of adrenaline through Gary and would make the actual first piercing just a little more intense because of it.

Ben pulled the skin of Gary's scrotum outward, pressing it against the foam core, then he deftly slid the first needle through the skin and into the board. The needle angled slightly outward to prevent it pulling out unexpectedly. Gary's reaction was surprisingly less dramatic. He didn't cry out or moan, just a sharp intake of breath.

Ben pressed his forearm against Gary's forehead again, waiting for his breathing to slow a little, then he unwrapped another needle. Pulling the cap off he again showed the needle to Gary, and this time Gary spoke.

"Oh God. Oh God." Gary was smiling slightly but also very nervous.

Ben smiled back with an innocence that can only cover mischief. He the pulled the skin of Gary's scrotum out on the opposite side and slid another needle through. This time Gary yelped a little, sounding more like a toy poodle than a human.

Ben placed his forearm on Gary's brow again. That is the way it progressed, each needle shown to Gary before being inserted into the skin of his scrotum and afterward a comforting gesture by Ben. The scene developed a slow rhythm, broken only by Gary's vocalizations.

About the tenth needle Gary looked at Ben and spoke. "Oh God, I'm fucked now."

Ben nodded in agreement and slid another needle through the skin of Gary's scrotum and into the foam core. Then he looked at Gary and spoke, "breathe."

Gary breathed, he had been holding his breath since before the needle went in.

As I watched, I found myself very turned on by the simple yet incredibly painful scene. Gary's cock was about half hard, and though the skin of his scrotum was trying to retract, the needles held it in place securely.

Once Ben and finished putting about a dozen needles in each side of Gary's scrotum, he stopped. His arm rested on Gary's forehead and he looked into Gary's eyes.

"You want a picture of this? It's really pretty."

Gary smiled and nodded, pointing to the small digital camera he brought with him. Though there were special days reserved for photography during the event, most people didn't mind if you took pictures of your own scenes. Ben picked up the camera and took a couple of close-ups of his handiwork. Though Gary's balls would be none the worse for the wear after the scene, he would have his souvenir.

After a few minutes, Ben asked Gary if he was ready for the needles to come out. Gary cringed and nodded, expecting more pain as they were removed. I could see he was surprised as Ben took the first couple of needles out and put them in a nearby sharps container. This special plastic jug would keep the needles from accidentally sticking anyone later. Ben removed a third needle and slid it into the container. He did not re-cap the needles to avoid the possibility of an accidental stick.

The fourth needle he withdrew much slower and Gary winced. Ben wanted to savor the scene a little and he really enjoyed seeing men experiencing intense pain at his hands. I guess that is the mark of a true sadist?

He proceeded to pull the needles out and after he withdrew the last one, he turned to Gary again. Smiling and looking into Gary's eyes, he reached over to a spray bottle of alcohol.

Gary saw it from the corner of his eye and began pleading. "Oh no, please don't, Oh God, Oh God."

Ben looked at him with that sweet deceptive smile and shot a spray mist of alcohol directly onto Gary's recently pierced balls.

"FUCK! FUCK, FUCK, FUCK!" Gary yelled at the top of his lungs.

Ben chuckled and then pressed a fresh gauze pad against the skin of Gary's scrotum. The pad absorbed what little blood was leaking from the piercings. He patiently held the gauze in place and blotted until the bleeding stopped.

Gary calmed down and began laughing. His body was electrified with endorphins and adrenaline and he was almost euphoric.

Ben pulled the gauze away once the bleeding stopped and balled the bloody pad up in his hand, then he pulled the rubber glove off over the gauze and transferred the balled up glove to his other hand. He pulled he second glove off over the first making a neat latex encased bundle for the bloody gauze. After tossing it into the waste basket, he leaned down over Gary and hugged him tightly. They stayed that way for several minutes while Gary's breathing and heartbeat returned to normal.

I slowly backed away, giving them their privacy and returned to my room to process the scene I had just witnessed. Later I would ask Ben to do the same thing to me, and teach me how to do it to others. In the leather/SM scene sometimes it's best to have hands-on instruction, and to know exactly what something feels like before doing it to others.

The Doctor Is In

Growing up as the son of a doctor left its mark on me. Though my father was not an MD, but rather a research scientist, I still grew up around a hospital and all the accouterments that come with it. Our home had lots of medical castoffs in it including a pair of forceps that I used for many of my hobby projects. Later in life I would still find an attraction to medical supplies, especially those used in surgery. I guess it's because they are usually made of stainless steel and are shiny.

I also like foraging in hardware stores, especially one very good one we are blessed with in my hometown of Dallas. Scanning the aisles of that place is always fun, especially if you are kinky like me. There is always a big bargain bin of nifty tools right near the door, and that is where I found bins of surgical tools that could be adapted for other purposes. I am sure the owners of the store meant for woodworkers and do-it-yourselfers to make use of the tools but would have no idea that someone as kinky as me would find them useful as well.

In one of those bins I found miniature forceps. These little scissors-shaped clamps were about three inches long and had a locking ratchet as part of the handles. These gadgets allow surgeons to clamp off a blood vessel or grab some otherwise slippery bit during surgery. The problem with these was that they had very sharp teeth on them to make sure things didn't slip away. For my use those teeth could cause damage and it might be permanent. Still hey! They were shiny, and cheap!

I loaded up a bag with a couple of dozen of them and trotted to the checkout counter. Once I got home with my new toys, I began experimenting. I suspected they would be too intense for use on the skin, but without trying them I would never know. I first clipped one of the forceps to the skin between my thumb and forefinger. I have found this is a pretty good place to test clamps and clips.

"Motherfucker!"

OK, that definitely won't work on skin, unless you want it to be seriously bruised or injured. The mark the clamp left in my skin was bright red, and the impression wasn't going away anytime soon. That just confirmed what I had figured about use on skin, but I had to try anyway. I guess I had forgotten the truth about surgeons. They use those little clamps to pull skin out of the way. If they leave marks, well that's just more work for the plastic surgeons.

I put the clamps away in my toy box and figured some day I would find a way to use them. Little did I know that it would be the following night.

I was visiting a couple of friends for dinner. They were a delightful straight couple that I had known for several years. Sherry was a beautiful woman with raven black hair. She could have easily modeled as a Betty Paige look-alike. John, her husband, was a big guy with almost white blonde hair and lots of muscles. He had been in the military but now was in a consulting business, so his physique had suffered a little, but he was still attractive and well muscled.

They had invited me over for dinner, but John had told me that he wanted a chance to play with me. He had never done CBT with a man before and both he and his wife were eager to try it.

After dinner we relaxed a bit and swapped stories of kinky encounters, something leatherfolk seem to do much like fishermen. Our tales are of the ones we caught though, not the ones who got away! The conversation got a little thin and John finally got around to the big question. He asked me if I would try some CBT on him with his wife. John played mainly with women, but occasionally he got a chance to play with a man. Since he was mainly a Top, that meant using a whole different set of skills for some more specialized play. I knew John liked genitorture on women, and it was not a big jump to doing the same to men, with the exception of having some additional equipment to play with.

We moved to the couple's bedroom that had a big four poster bed. The frame was actually welded steel, and it had a variety of attachment points on the posts, including a set of eyebolts that were perfect for hanging a sling. If there was any doubt what John had in mind, the sling, neatly hung above the bed, eliminated any questions.

As John took off his clothes, I set up my toy box on a nearby dresser. Sherry watched as I opened the aluminum tool case that serves as one of my toy boxes. The case is neatly divided into compartments and each had a variety of toys in them, categorized by their intended use. Sherry had lots of questions, and I expected that she might be getting interested in CBT as well.

As I began laying out a few toys for what I had planned, Sherry picked up the plastic box containing the stash of forceps I had bought the day before.

"Oh my God! These look really intense," Sherry said, holding one of the forceps up for a closer inspection.

"They are," I assured her as I held up my hand, the mark still visible from my earlier experiment.

"How are you going to use these?"

I looked at her again, then plucked the forceps from her hand and put it back in the box.

"That may be for a more advanced session," I said as I snapped the plastic box closed.

By this time, John was naked in the sling. As I turned I was pleasantly surprised to see John, smiling with his legs spread, his ample cock already growing in anticipation. Now I know I would never have a chance for anything really sexual with John, besides I think my partner might object as well as his wife. That said, it was still fun to have a nice big, hunky straight man, buck-naked and in a sling offering his cock and balls to me for my use and amusement. Sometimes I really love what I do!

As I took a good look at his cock, I saw that he had a good-sized crop of golden pubic hair surrounding it. For me, pubic hair is a turn on. Though shaved genitals are sometimes easier to work with for CBT, pubic hair offers its own unique properties. Personally, I think the feeling of the hairs actually makes some things more intense for the bottom.

As Sherry looked back to my toy box and absent mindedly fingered the plastic box containing the forceps, I was struck with a singularly twisted idea. Though they might not work for the skin, there were lots of other places hey could be used...at least with all that pubic hair!

To Sherry's delight I once again lifted the box of forceps. John watched, curious as to what I had in mind. I asked Sherry to hold the box and be my assistant, meanwhile I moved closer to John and reached out and grasped his steadily hardening penis. It was pretty huge, I had to admit and the weight of his organ as it engorged with blood gave me a tingle. I stroked it a few times, just for good measure and then turned to Sherry.

"He's got a really nice one doesn't he?" She beamed.

"Oh yes," I agreed. "It's a very nice cock, and I would hate to damage it with these forceps."

John raised an eyebrow as I took the first forceps and approached his crotch. I carefully opened the clamp and then positioned it near the base of his cock, and clamped it down tight on a couple of pubic hairs. As I released it, it dangled down and tugged at the hairs.

"Ouch!" John tried to see what I was doing but couldn't.

Sherry smiled and chuckled with glee, she knew where this was headed.

I then took another clamp and attached it to some hairs on the opposite side of his cock. Of course I took the opportunity to stroke his cock a few more times, just to reward him…and myself.

I followed in the same manner until I had used all the forceps and they hung in an even if crowded pattern around his cock and balls. Some even hung from the hair growing from his scrotum, something I know was pretty annoying and painful. Once I was done, I stood back and admired my handiwork.

Sherry was fascinated with the forest of dangling clamps and she prodded them a bit, making them clang against one another.

"Sort of like wind chimes," I chuckled. Then, I nudged the clamps again making them tinkle a little louder. At the sound, John started laughing. He swung in the sling back and forth a bit, making the forceps jingle again. From his smile, I could tell that the repeated painful sensations caused by the pulling of his pubic hairs had started a little of his body's natural painkillers flowing.

I tugged at some of the clamps, causing John's smile to be replaced by a grimace. After amusing myself a bit more, I turned to Sherry.

"I really want to thank you for giving me the inspiration on how to use those forceps."

Sherry smiled, "All in the interest of science."

I turned to my toy box and opened a small plastic box. Inside was a length of nylon cord that I often used for cock bondage. As I approached John with it he smiled, expecting me to start tying his genitals up. Instead I threaded the cord through the looped handles of the forceps. They jingled louder as I completed stringing all the clamps together. Holding the cord, I tugged it gently. John winced and then looked into my eyes.

"You are not going to do what I think you are going to do, are you?"

I smiled back in my most innocent smile. "What did you think I was going to do?"

Before he could answer I took both ends of the cord and jerked them towards my chest.

"This?"

John stifled a scream. Sherry gasped.

The cord had neatly pulled all the forceps away from John's body, and each carried with them a tiny tuft of pubic hair. The jingled as they now hung free from his crotch.

Once John caught his breath, he looked at me. Sweat was dripping from his forehead and he was still shaking a bit from the extreme pain.

"Damn, you are a sadistic bastard."

"I'll take that as a compliment," I said as I moved beside him and laid a hand on his chest.

Sherry was glowing as she stroked John's still hard cock. "I guess this still needs attention?"

John looked down at her as she was slipping the head of his big dick into her mouth.

"I guess with every pain there needs to be a little pleasure?" I said as I gently stroked John's chest, grazing his nipples. He took another sharp intake of breath, but this time it was not in pain. Seems John also had very sensitive nipples, and while Sherry was taking care of his cock, I satisfied myself by playing with his now erect nipples. I do love nipple torture, but that is another story.

He Could Have Been a Contender

When you have been around the leather/fetish/BDSM community for a while, you sometimes feel a little jaded. You think you have seen everything and there is nothing new under the sun. That is usually the time I find myself pleasantly surprised by a type of play I have never seen before. It is those times that reinvigorate me and make me realize that there are so many possibilities in the expressions of human sexuality that I will never see them all. It is especially true in the leather/fetish/BDSM community.

I am a member of several groups whose main purpose is to educate and inform our community, but I am also a member in a few whose main purpose is strictly to provide a safe place for leatherfolk to play. One of those groups is a men's playgroup. Its sole purpose is to provide a place where men, no matter what their sexual orientation, can engage in safe, sane and consensual BDSM activities.

Our parties happen once a month at a local "public" dungeon/art gallery. Because of the strange laws here in Texas, we do not have dungeons, but rather galleries where performance art can be exhibited. Most of the events are private, so the whole "art thing" is not necessary, but for the proprietors of the establishments it's just what they have to do. Go figure?

It was at one of these parties that I watched a couple of friends engaged in a scene that really opened my eyes to an activity in which I had only been mildly involved. A lot of the guys in the group like rough body play. That means punching and kicking to those unfamiliar with the term. It sounds kind of odd, but it really stems from those macho schoolyard "trading punches" sessions so many boys engage in.

It is not uncommon to see a couple of big muscled guys trading punches and slaps against their beefy pecs, thighs and just about any other major muscle mass. They go away bruised and in pain, but usually laughing from the whole "rough house" experience. Though I enjoy punching as part of a scene, I usually don't get into the trading punches type play because I am a wimp. Well, not really a wimp, but I just hate getting punched. Consequently, I do most of my punching with the bottom securely bound to avoid retaliation. As one of my friends says, I am a "delicate Top".

I had heard about *ball punching* for years and had even learned to do it on a few play partners who enjoyed it. The kind of punching I am talking about is really not a full on left hook or anything pugilistic, but rather a firm blow delivered to the perineum. That is the area behind the balls, and between the legs sometimes called the "taint". "Taint your ass and taint your balls," is the colloquial expression.

Striking this area lets the body absorb most of the force of the blow, but still delivers a sound slap to the testicles. Now before you haul off and start jamming your fist into your partner's nuts, a word of warning. It can be very dangerous and painful if you don't do it right. Additionally, it takes practice and instruction from an experienced Top or bottom to really do it right. A strong blow to the testicles can result in a painful injury, swelling of the balls and sometimes more permanent damage to your reproductive system. Consider yourself warned!

Most men can stand a slap or two to the balls if it is not too strong. The reaction to a strong blow to the balls can result in an involuntary contraction of the gut, resulting in an instant replay of anything eaten prior to the scene. In other words some guys react to having their balls racked by vomiting. Not my idea of a pretty scene, and usually a party stopper.

Now, with all that information tucked soundly away in your head, I will tell you about the scene my friends did at the party.

Both guys had been joking and trading punches to the chest. Each time they did so, you could hear a resounding thump and a little gasp as they almost knocked the breath out of each other. After a few dozen blows both guys were pretty filled with adrenaline, and horny as hell.

They retired to the back of the dungeon where they traded kisses and less violent gropes. Before long one man was naked and hanging in a sling while his partner continued to kiss and fondle him.

Watching them, I figured it wouldn't be long before Gary, the guy in the sling would be getting a nice helping of Rod's cock, but I was wrong. At least for the time being.

Rod began using his hands to play with Gary's cock and balls. He stroked, squeezed and teased him mercilessly. Gary was more than a little turned on, and by the look in his eyes I could tell he was ready for anything Rod could dish out.

Rod took Gary's balls in his big hands and pulled them away from Gary's body. His fingers encircled the tops of the testicles and pulled the scrotum downward like a ball stretcher. The great thing about using your hands for CBT is that there is always intimate contact. Hands are so much more sensual than a metal ring or leather strap.

As Rod tugged on Gary's balls, Gary began moaning. It was a primal sound that came from the depths of Gary's soul, and it was sexy as hell. I moved close enough to watch but far enough away to allow the two men personal space. Was I rude to watch?

Hell no, they were playing at a party of leathermen. What did they expect? I also suspect that the exhibitionist aspect of the whole scene was working for them as well. Both men were handsome and very well built. They were used to people staring at them.

As Rod pulled Gary's balls, the sling began to swing. Rod was swinging Gary back and forth using only the tension on his balls. Rod let the sling slow down, but still maintained a firm grip on his partner's nuts. Then he leaned down and brought his face very close to Gary's stretched balls. I thought he was going to lick them, but instead he ran his rough two-day growth of beard over the stretched surface of Gary's scrotum.

Gary moaned again and squirmed as Rod's prickly beard scraped across Gary's balls like sandpaper. While there, Rod took the opportunity to give Gary's hardening cock a couple of quick licks, but I got the impression he was saving anything more amorous until later.

As Rod backed away from Gary's crotch, he looked the hot man right in the eye and then delivered a short slap to Gary's balls. Gary gasped and then growled with another of those primal sounds he was making earlier. Rod paused, watching Gary process the sensation and then he slapped his balls again. His hand swept up between Gary's legs and smacked the scrotum on the underside, delivering most of the bow to Gary's perineum.

Again Gary groaned and growled. Then he looked Rod in the eyes and muttered, "yessss".

Rod nodded and smiled. With just that simple communication the two men had negotiated the scene. Sometimes, that is all it takes for experienced players to come to an agreement.

Rod curled his fingers into a fist and with the back of his hand facing upward, he again brought an upward blow to Gary's hanging balls. This time a little more of the force was delivered to the testicles rather than the perineum. Gary moaned and shook his head like he was shaking off something from his face. Rod watched and once Gary had focused on him again he drew back his hand again. This time he stopped just short of striking Gary and he watched Gary flinch as he anticipated the blow.

Gary realized he had been fooled and shot Rod an evil grin just about the time Rod connected with a surprise punch. Gary groaned and then growled at Rod, "Motherfucker!"

"Surprise!" Rod beamed. The he gave Gary's nuts another lighter smack.

Gary grimaced and then looked at Rod with a sparkle in his eyes. "You hit like a girl."

Rod raised an eyebrow and got the message that Gary wanted more. The group of men watching tried to stifle their laughter at Gary's remark but a few chuckles leaked through.

The energy of the scene was contagious. All of us who watched were not only interested in the scene but highly aroused by it. You could almost taste the testosterone in the air. More than a few of the observers were fondling their crotches and some were openly stroking their cocks.

Rod started back in on Gary's equipment. He smacked his balls a few more times with upward blows between the legs, but nothing too hard. Gary was continuing to groan and occasionally taunt Rod, sending a clear signal that he was enjoying the scene.

After a few more blows, Rod changed his technique. He started a series of rapid fire slaps to Gary's balls. Each one a little harder and faster. Gary's vocalizations got louder with each contact, his moans began to sound more like a siren. The tone and volume was getting higher pitched and louder with each blow.

Then Rod stopped and waited for Gary to process the intense pain. The room was silent. Only Gary's breathing could be heard. As it returned to more normal cadence, I saw him look directly in Rod's eyes. That was apparently his signal to start again.

Rod began again, this time using his fist to slap Gary's dangling balls over and over again, faster and faster. Gary's voice had twisted from a moan into a genuine scream by the time Rod paused again. He was panting roughly and his eyes looked more animalistic than human.

Rod reached down and grabbed Gary's cock. It was still a little engorged even after the pummeling his balls had taken. Rod squeezed it hard and Gary closed his eyes.

"Aw, fuck yes." Gary whimpered.

Rod stroked Gary's penis a few times and then let it flop against his abdomen. He curled his hand into a fist again and held it up so Gary could see it. Gary nodded and Rod began again.

The whole party had gathered around the scene taking place. With the number of men stroking themselves and each other, the whole thing looked like something from a Tom of Finland drawing. Lots of hunky men and lots of sexual energy.

Rod used the same technique as he had before of bringing Gary to a crescendo of sensation with a series of steadily faster and more intense blows. By now, he was punching Gary's nuts like a prizefighter, though the actual force of each blow was carefully measured to avoid any permanent injury.

After a couple of more sequences, it was clear that Gary was exhausted. Rod stopped his punching and moved to Gary's head. He leaned over and kissed Gary deeply and held his face in his hands. Gary's cock responded to the affection with a slight twitch and was soon erect.

Rod let his hands travel down Gary's smooth chest and abdomen to his crotch again. This time, instead of punching, he took Gary's balls in his hands and gently massaged them. Gary moaned again. The trauma delivered to his balls made them very sensitive, and Rod was enjoying seeing him squirm. He was also aware of the nice hard cock that was bobbing above Gary's balls. Rod stroked it a few more times before he leaned down and ran his rough beard over the head of Gary's throbbing penis.

By now several of the men watching were actively engaged in stroking each other, and as Rod resumed stroking Gary, they moved in closer. Gary's eyes watched Rod and the others and I saw his face take on an expression of pure animal lust.

He reached out to one of the men nearby and grabbed the man's exposed dick. In no time another man offered his cock to Gary's other hand. I could tell Gary was in heaven as he eagerly stroked both men while Rod took care of him.

Most of our parties don't descend into the kind of sex charged scene that had happened around Rod and Gary, but it was an experience I will always fondly remember. I think it is the kind of thing that keeps me from becoming blasé about the leather/fetish/ BDSM community. What we do as leatherfolk may not always lead to sex, but it is always sexual in nature. If it's not, you must not be doing it right!

Truly Shocking

Of all the recent innovations in sex toys, the field of electro-torture and electro-stimulation has grown the most rapidly. It seems every month a new electrical gadget comes to the market and unfortunately the prices seem to be getting higher.

Now, before anyone calls me on this, I want to say that a lot of these toys are really fun to play with. The sophisticated electro-stimulation units now available have lots of nifty settings and even come in remote control models. I have a friend who bought a big unit that interfaces with his laptop for a truly geek-sex experience.

Most of these toys are variations on the TENS unit. For those who may not know, TENS is an acronym for Transcutaneous Electrical Nerve Stimulator. A big term for a gadget that sends an electric charge through your skin. This charge is sent in the form of pulses that are controlled via frequency, intensity and wave-form. These devices were originally developed in the mid-70s and were used to relieve pain and are still in use today. They grew from an early 1950's fad called the Relaxicisor. This was a device that caused a person's muscles to contract when stimulated with an electrical current. Supposedly they would give you the benefits of exercise without any work. I actually tried one of these old units and they are fun to play with, however they do nothing to "spot reduce" or genuinely build muscles.

TENS units or electrostimulators should never be used on individuals who have implanted pacemakers, since the electrical current may disturb the function of the pacemaker. No pacemaker equals no heartbeat and that would be a bad thing!

The sex toy versions are essentially the same devices, just without the medical cache. They have been available since the mid-80's as kinky toys. My first electrotorture machine was called a Folsom Box. It still works and for my money it's as good as any of the newer more advanced models, with the exception that it does not have as many settings and variations of pulse. Still, they can be very effective and I would not give mine up for anything.

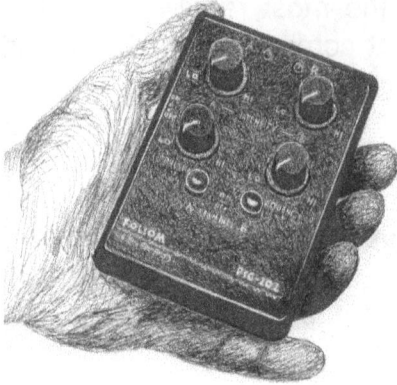

Delivering the electric current to the body is where the real fun comes, especially if you like to collect toys or have a good case of do-it-yourself fever. TENS units use adhesive conductive pads to send the pulses through the skin. These are special rubber pads impregnated with a conductive material and coated with an adhesive that not only sticks them to the skin but acts as an electrolyte, guaranteeing good contract and transmission of the current.

Most of the sex toys for use in CBT are made of metal or other conductive material and must be used with a special conductive lubricant. This water-based lube has an electrolyte built into it to assure good contact. Without this lube, the sensation delivered is a burn, and you can get actual burns on the skin if it is not properly lubricated.

The sensation these gadgets cause ranges from a mild tingling to a severe zap that causes the muscles to contract. The actual sensation can vary greatly depending on the frequency and intensity of the device. Experimentation is the best way to learn how to use a TENS or electro-stimulation toy. The other nice thing about electric toys is that you can use them on yourself with ease, allowing you to get a chance to experience what they do first hand, so to speak.

This all leads to a nice little scene I had with a friend of mine while experimenting with some new toys. Mike is a Top now, but he began his leather life as a bottom. Having had the experience as a bottom, there are some things he still enjoys and Mike loves CBT. Unfortunately, a lot of people don't understand Tops enjoying bottoming occasionally and because of this, it makes it difficult to get those urges met. Personally, although I have never been a bottom or boy or slave, I still enjoy a good thuddy flogging occasionally. Why? It feels great, and really gets me going.

Mike dropped by one afternoon to help me try out a few new toys I had picked up. About a year ago, I had my large toy chest stolen from my truck. I guess the thieves thought it was a tool chest. I can imagine their disappointment when they found it contained only an assortment of BDSM toys. The result of the theft was that I had to replace a large number of my toys. An expensive proposition, but it afforded me the chance to update a few things.

I had replaced my old Folsom Box with a similar model and had purchased a few other electrical toys, including a variety of conductive cock rings and electrical contacts. The latest purchase came from an electronics store. There are conductive elastic wrist bands made for people working on electronic parts. These are designed to attach to a grounded source to prevent static discharges, which can damage delicate circuits. These can also be modified with the addition of a suitable plug for use as CBT toys.

I had purchased four of the wrist bands and attached the correct plugs to them for my use.

Since the electro-stimulation device has two channels, the four bands could be used as alternating positive and negative contacts.

Now Mike was volunteering his personal equipment to test out my modifications. There wasn't much ceremony to the whole thing, since Mike and I had played often before and he was as interested as I was in seeing what the new bands would do. He stripped out of his clothes and lay down on the floor. I had the Folsom Box already out and the modified wristbands ready.

Since I wanted to try them on an erect cock, I asked Mike to put on a leather cock ring first and he had stroked himself to a fully aroused condition before I put the bands on. My plan was to use all four bands on his ample penis. They would be positioned evenly along the shaft, and connected in pairs that would allow me to single out either the end or the base of his penis.

I coated Mike's cock with a thin layer of electrogel lubrication. The added stimulation helped to maintain his erection as well. Besides, it was fun stroking his big cock. Then I began putting the

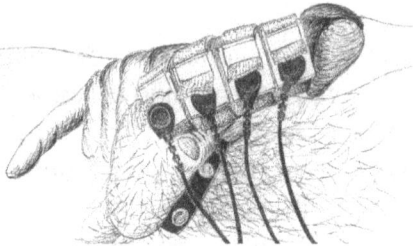

elastic bands on his cock. They fit loosely but had adjustable tabs to allow tightening. Once all four bands were on and tight, I attached the wires from them to the sockets in the electro-stimulation box. Mike watched and smiled.

Once everything was attached I looked at Mike and turned on the box. The power lights blinked on and we were ready. I made sure the controls were turned to the lowest settings, to avoid any surprises when I activated the box. Since it operated on a 9-volt battery, there was little chance it could do any harm, but I always like to avoid accidents.

I turned on both channels and slowly eased the dial on the intensity control of channel one up. When I got to about 5 on the dial Mike began to respond.

"Interesting," Mike said.

"Interesting? Does that mean you like it?"

"Well I can feel it, a tingling in the end of my cock. Not a bad feeling," Mike said as he looked down at his cock.
I then turned the frequency slowly upward and watched his reaction. When I got to about 4, he closed his eyes.

"On yea," Mike said. "That's pretty good right there."

Now I moved the pulse control to a point where the light was flashing about once every second. The pulses were making his cock jump in time to the flashing light on the box. I slowly moved the pulse rate higher and his cock jumped faster. I then brought it back down to the previous setting.

"Now time for number 2." I slowly turned up the power on the second channel and Mike stiffened.

"Oh yea!"

His cock was twitching stronger and his hands were clutching the rug.

"So that feels OK?"

"Oh, hell yes!"

I watched him twitch for a while and then tried modifying the settings again. The higher the power the more he twitched.

"Feels like there are a thousand little needles surrounding my dick," Mike said. "Not painful, just really good."

Next I decided to try a little experiment. I used the switches for each channel to turn them on and off. I alternated channels so the first pulse would go to the base of Mike's cock and the second would go the head. I switched them back and forth and watched his reaction.

Mike began writhing. His hips were jerking off the floor like he was fucking an invisible person. I took that as a positive sign. When I stopped he relaxed a little.

"That felt like some electrical hand was stroking my cock," Mike panted. "If you hadn't stopped I would have shot my load right there."

I took that as a challenge and began again. This time I slowly eased the power up and the frequency down a little. For some reason the intensity at lower frequencies seems to make the body respond better, or at least stronger.

I began alternating the channels again in time to the pulses, and slowly increased the speed of the pulse rate. Mike again began bucking up from the floor with each pulse. It looked like he was fucking the air, but I knew it was the electrical tingling that was making his body respond.

This time I decided not to stop and just see if I could get a full blown orgasm from him without touching his cock. I kept up the stimulation and watched as his breathing became faster and faster. His cock was twitching like some unseen had was stroking it.

In a few more seconds he clenched his fists and arched his back. His cock was still twitching to the pulses of the machine as it shot a stream of cum several inches into the air. I let the pulses continue for a while as his orgasm subsided. Finally his hips fell back to the floor.

Seeing this, I stopped the device and turned it off. Mike was still panting and slightly incoherent, but I knew he enjoyed the "test".

"So any comments for our user survey?"

Mike laughed and turned his sweatty face to me. "I laughed, I cried. It was better than *Cats*."

Tug Of War

I do a lot of workshops around the country that explore cock and ball torture. They are designed to encourage people to enhance their sex lives with CBT and share their ideas. I often get a lot of very useful tips from the people attending these workshops. Sometimes, the workshop itself becomes a really imaginative scene. This is usually not through some conscious effort on my part, but strictly on the shared energy and imagination of those attending.

At one such event I had been doing what has become my usual presentation. During it I encourage men in the audience to participate and volunteer to help out with demonstrations. Sometimes I get very little response. Men are notoriously shy, and if it means exposing their genitals, even more so. I suspect a lot of this has to do with the myths of size equaling prowess and masculinity. Many men would not want to be exposed as having a smaller cock than another man!

At this particular workshop I was blessed with several good looking exhibitionistic guys who had absolutely no problem stripping down and letting me use their equipment for demonstration purposes. The energy of the attendees was pretty good, and even though it was a mix of both men and women, straight and gay, everyone was in a really playful and uninhibited mood.

Toward the end of the session, I was showing how to make a ball stretcher using rope. I had the braided nylon rope tied securely around a volunteer's scrotum, his balls stretched and smooth from the tension. The extra rope hung between his legs and I picked up the ends to demonstrate how this specific tie could be used to tug him wherever I wanted.

As I was doing it, he pulled back in a show of resistance. He liked the feeling of weight pulling against his balls. The group laughed at his resistance and I made a big show of fighting against him. That's when it struck me. Maybe that fight could be turned into a scene. I proposed a challenge to the man whose balls I had at the end of the rope. A contest with another man.

He smiled and the group erupted in the chant "tug of war, tug of war." As I said, the energy was very playful!

There was a second guy, still naked from an earlier demonstration, sitting on the floor in front of the first row of chairs. I looked over to him and asked if he'd be up for a challenge and he jumped to his feet.

I tied the same ball stretcher on him. It consisted of a rope run up the area between the balls. At the top of the scrotum, where the penis begins, I wrapped a loop of rope and threaded it under the end running up his scrotum. Doubling it back, I continued wrapping the rope snugly around the top of his scrotum. Each warp was carefully layered next to the previous one, taking care not to pinch any skin. After four or five wraps, his balls were sufficiently stretched, and I tied the end of the rope to the length running up the balls. This kept the knot on the lower portion of his scrotum and assured any weight would be evenly distributed up the coiled rope.

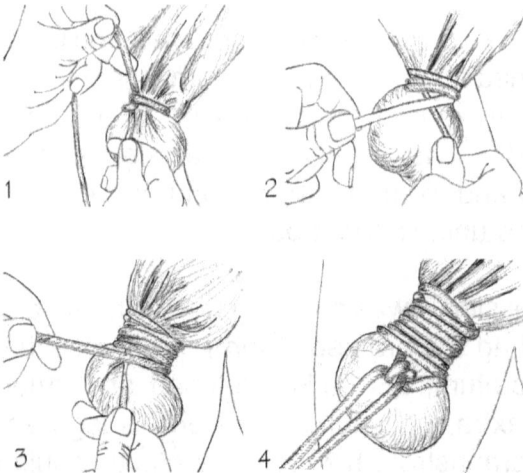

All I had to do now was to tie the ends of his rope to the other man's rope and they would be linked. After making sure the knots were secure I had the men separate until the rope was taught. The two men stepped back and pulled the rope, their balls extending away from their bodies, bringing it taught. I told each of them that if they felt too much pain or were afraid of injury to yield to the other and the contest would be over. The group started to cheer them on, but I interrupted them before the contest could start.

"If this is going to really be a contest, we need a way to determine who wins. So I need an impartial judge to help out."

I looked around the room and found several eager faces, however for this game I needed someone who was a little reluctant. Sitting in the third row I found my judge. She was a middle-aged woman, wearing what appeared to be ordinary street clothes. The only hint at fetishwear was the pair of spike-heeled shoes she wore. I asked if she would agree to help and she nodded.

I brought her up to the front and told her that the best way to find who won was to get close enough to really see the action. As I spoke I picked up a pillow that I had used earlier on a demonstration and placed it on the floor directly below the suspended rope. I asked her to lay down with her head directly under the rope, so she could accurately measure who won.

The group got even rowdier with this suggestion. She blushed slightly and then accepted my invitation. Lying on the floor, she was looking up at the rope and at two handsome men's balls stretched above her. I do feel a little guilty for any humilliation she might have felt, but I also knew she was enjoying the view.

To assure that she could accurately measure the test, I hung a marker on the rope. The group broke into a roar of laughter. The fact that the marker was a battery operated vibrator may have contributed to that laughter.

I told her to watch and whenever the vibrator moved past either of her shoulders, she was to signal the winner. To do this, I gave her a small plastic whistle I carried in my toy bag.

By now the group was standing and rooting for their favorites. I signaled the start of the contest with a countdown and was joined by almost everyone in the room.

"Four, three, two, one!"

Both men began to pull in earnest on the rope and the group went wild. Cheering like it was a professional football game. Some even chanted their favorite's names. I watched the men's faces as they genuinely strained at the rope. Neither was pulling too hard, since any pressure would be felt by both of them. They grimaced and groaned, but really tried their best. The vibrator moved left and right getting closer and closer to the judge's shoulders, but not ever going beyond.

Finally, I saw a pained expression on one man's face and he yielded slightly. It was enough for the other to pull the vibrator past the judge's shoulder and she blew the whistle loudly.

Cheers erupted from the group, as the men stepped closer to let the tension off the rope. I helped my volunteer judge to her feet and held the winners hand up in victory.

All in all it was a silly contest, but it was a very good way to demonstrate the variety of fun you could have with CBT. More importantly, it was fun for the group watching and all three participants. The other lesson from this little game was that no expensive toys were required. Just a couple of pieces of rope, a vibrator, and the collective imagination of a group of kinky people were all it took to create a memorable scene that was talked about for weeks.

Great Balls of Fire

I love the 4th of July. I have fond memories of spending the day with my friends in the backyard detonating firecrackers all afternoon. We exploded them until the ringing in our ears was constant. I suspect it did some permanent damage, but nothing severe.

The big event was always after dinner. Usually a group of neighbors would gather and have a cookout and then the parents would get out their fireworks. The big stuff that only worked at night. Fountains, roman candles, skyrockets and more.

When I was younger, I got sparklers. I learned how to handle then safely, and without burning myself or my friends. The hot wires left over after the sparklers ran out always went into a coffee can of water. Since my parents liked fireworks too, they taught me how to use them safely.

Now, the only fireworks I see are shot by professionals. Local laws have outlawed even the tame stuff, and since I don't know anyone with a big enough piece of land outside the city, I have to be content with watching.

There is one exception of course, and that is the sparklers. You can still buy them if you drive out of the city limits, and since they don't throw huge fireballs into the sky or make any noise, no one has ever complained.

What I remember about sparklers was how interesting the sparks felt. Occasionally they would fall on my hands and they didn't burn, they just felt like little grains of sand. They left no residue and bounced off the skin. I would never hold them too close, but at a distance of a couple of feet, the feeling was very interesting.

Sometimes childhood memories make the best fodder for adult fun. I was attending a picnic a few years ago on the 4th with a group of kinky friends. We had made home-made ice cream and cooked lots of burgers and hotdogs. It was a sedate gathering until darkness fell.

Because of the location of the party, we could easily see one of the professional fireworks shows in the distance being shot from a public park. Sitting around after dinner smoking a cigar and watching the fireworks gave me an idea. I had my toy box with me and though no play was planned I decided to improvise.

A good friend who had helped me out in a workshop demo was present and I asked if he would be interested in an experiment. Danny's eyes lit up and then he asked, "and would it involve doing something to my private areas?"

My smile gave the answer away and he agreed. We found a spot near the swimming pool in the back yard and I told him to wait while I got my toys. Danny set his lemonade down and sat in one of the patio chairs near the pool. By the time I had gotten back, Danny was already naked, sitting on his towel. I handed him a fresh cigar, which he accepted as a token of appreciation for his help. As he lit it I began to unpack and explain what I wanted to try. The nice thing about the back yard was the nice high privacy fence that would prevent any prying eyes from observing our play. There was also the matter of the neighbors being present at the party. Sometimes it helps to live in a kinky neighborhood!

I had Danny sit on one of the wrought-iron patio chairs. I fastened his legs to the legs of the chair with some short lengths of rope. The bondage was perfunctory, since Danny was eager to try the experiment, but I didn't want his legs accidentally getting in the way of any possible danger.

Once he was positioned, I pulled out the small fire extinguisher

I carried. This also piqued his interest but he didn't say a word. Danny just smiled and puffed his cigar. Next I removed a couple of boxes of sparklers that I had picked up for the occasion. Though they were technically fireworks, they would draw no attention behind the privacy fence. Besides, the fire department and police were looking for much more dangerous stuff.

As I opened the box, I noticed Danny's cock begin to harden. I looked at it for a second, and then up to Danny. "Doesn't take much to get you going does it?"

"Heck, you had me getting a chubby with the fire extinguisher." Danny blew a smoke ring and smiled.

It is great having twisted friends!

I told Danny to lean back and enjoy. Then I took one of the sparklers and lit it with my cigar lighter. Since it has a blow torch style flame, it made lighting the sparkler much easier than with a match.

As the long rod of aluminum filings began to sputter it attracted the attention of a few visitors who moved closer to watch. I have to admit I am a bit of a showman and Danny was an exhibitionist, so an audience was no problem for either of us.

The sparkler flared to full life and began trailing a cascade of white sparks. The tiny bits of aluminum are actually fine power that is slowed by the binder and oxidizer that makes them burn. These seemingly safe fireworks actually account for a great number of injuries. Usually it comes from people being burned by the hot wire. I would never touch anyone with that end, I only let the sparks that flew from the firework actually fall on skin. The sparks that emanate from the sparkler are relatively tame. You can pass your hand through them with little effect, and that was my inspiration.

I moved the sparkler over Danny's cock and balls. About 12 inches away the sparks were almost cool by the time they fell on his skin, but the scintillating feeling was profound. Danny's cock jumped at the touch of the sparks. Actually it was the mere proximity that made him twitch. I was careful to hold the sparkler in front of his cock, just incase any large particles fell off. I wanted his equipment in good shape!

I would move the sparkler to various positions between his legs, letting him savor the different feelings. As the sparkler burned near the end, I used it to light another. This was the best way to light them.

By now several people had gathered and were laughing and watching as I teased Danny's cock with the firework. I looked over my shoulder and saw my friend Mistress. She had been in town for the holiday and was staying with friends. She gave me a knowing wink. I motioned her to come over.

As she arrived I handed her the sparkler and asked her to attend to Danny for a moment while I got a special surprise.

"You won't have to ask me twice for that!" She took the sparkler and continued teasing Danny while I got a surprise from my bag. I had a supply of "flash cotton" with me. From my days as an amateur magician I had collected some pretty fun supplies. Flash Cotton was one of them. It is actually nitrocellulose or gun cotton. This low-level explosive is used by magicians to produce the bright yellow flashes of fire in their act. It burns at a relatively low temperature, relatively low for an explosive that is. The stuff can be dangerous if packed into a confined space. When ignited in the open, it burns very quickly and is safe enough to be held on the palm of the hand.

Here is where the warning comes.

Do not ever hold flash cotton in your fist or have any part of your or any other person's anatomy over it. Heat rises and therefore it will burn you severely if ignited below you. On your open hand or open skin, its heat rises rapidly and no burns will result. There are cases of people being burned with flash cotton but these are usually very minor and only slightly redden the skin, usually much less severe than a sunburn.

So back to the pool party…

I took a small bit of flash cotton and twisted it into a thin string about 4 inches long. As I watched Danny, he was leaned back, puffing his cigar with his eyes closed enjoying the sensations. I took the moment to add the final touch. I motioned to Mistress to move the sparkler away for a moment while I laid the flash cotton string on the area just above Danny's fully erect cock. Since he was leaning back in the chair, his abdomen was almost parallel to the ground, and no part of his body was above it.

I told him not to move, and he opened his eyes just as I finished laying the flash cotton string on him. The sparkler was about to go out as I took it from Mistress, but there was still sufficient life left in it to ignite the flash cotton. There was a bright yellow flash! Danny jerked, his eyes blinked open as he let out a loud, "wow!" The people around us had a similar reaction and their gasps soon gave way to applause.

I put the spent sparkler into a coffee can being used for cigar butts, untied Danny's legs and helped him to his feet. He was still jittery from the surprise, but from the looks of his pubic area he was none the worse for the wear.

With all the dignity he could muster, Danny bowed then took Mistress hand and mine and we all bowed again. The group whooped and cheered and that was the moment Danny chose to push me into the pool.

Luckily I was wearing shorts and a T-shirt, wet leather would be a real painful scene.

On Target

One of the things that I find enjoyable about traveling to leather/ fetish events is the opportunity to talk to a wide variety of people. When I do CBT workshops, I get some really wonderful comments and ideas, and I find that people are more than willing to share stories of their own play with me. That's all part of what makes the leather/fetish/BDSM community so great.

At a recent event, I had a chance to have lunch with a group of folks who told me a great CBT story. This group was comprised mainly of women, and their favorite activity was having a male friend attend one of their little gatherings. Their kink was something known as CFNM, clothed female naked male (acronyms seem to be part of the leather/fetish scene as well). It is really a kind of group Femdom (female dominance) activity where a willing guy is relieved of his clothes in a room full of fully dressed women. The humiliation and embarrassment of his nudity is the turn on for both the women and the man. Additionally, this group liked to add a little more spice. They would tie up the willing male participant and play consensual BDSM games with him.

At one of these parties the women came up with a very unusual and creative game which I have since used in CBT workshops.

The party took place on a Saturday night. All of the women arrived at the hostess' house around 8:00pm and enjoyed refreshments and snacks while waiting for their male subject. James arrived at 9:00pm as he had been told. Once he got there, they had a surprise for him. James was told he was to be both the prize and the object of a game they wanted to play. Knowing that this game would undoubtedly involve him being naked, and since James really loved this kind of scene, he quickly agreed.

He was told to go into the back bedroom and remove all his clothes. Once naked, he was to return to the living room for the game. Whenever he was not following orders from the Hostess or her guests, James was told to stand straight with his hands clasped behind his back, his head bowed in submission. The Hostess told James he would not have to do anything he was unwilling to do. If there was something he felt was beyond his abilities or conscience, he was to say, "I am sorry, but I cannot do that, Mam." Those were to be his safe-words for the evening. Though the guests might be disappointed, they would respect his limits.

When he had removed his clothes, he walked back to the living room. He was blushing before he entered the room. Being naked with one woman was a lot different than being naked in front of a half-dozen. To make matters worse, the embarrassment was working in a perverse way to excite him as well. The humiliation quotient went up almost as fast as his erect cock.

He was handed a tray of drinks by the Hostess and told to serve the guests. Flushed with a warm glow, James began making his way around the room. As he offered the drinks to the female guests, they each remarked on his naked state. Some even made references to his still erect cock. The talk and laughter at the party was getting louder by the minute as James finished his duties and returned the tray to his Hostess.

She took the serving tray and stashed it in the kitchen before turning to lead James back into the room full of women. She told them to all take seats because the games were about to begin. James stood submissively behind her, his hands clasped behind his back as he had been instructed. The hostess handed each guest a handfull of rubber bands. These were the ordinary kind found in any office supply store.

She then turned and reached behind the sofa. There she had

hidden a surprise. In her hands was a piece of 1/4" plywood about two feet square. The wood had been sanded smooth and painted white. At the center of the plywood square was a 1½" hole with a target painted around it. It didn't take long for the guests to figure out what was going in the target!

The Hostess moved to James and told him to step forward. She had him hold the plywood target at his waist, with the hole positioned directly over his cock and balls. With a little patience, the Hostess managed to work James' balls through the hole, followed by his cock which had softened a bit. Once through the opening his equipment was framed by the circles of the target and he began to stiffen again.

The hostess explained that the guests would be allowed to shoot their rubber bands at the target until they had exhausted their supply, or until one of them managed to send a rubber band around James' cock. Whoever did this would get an extra prize!

The women were giddy with excitement and gathered around in front of their target. As the Hostess positioned James, she reached down and gave his stiff rod a friendly squeeze.

"Try not to move too much, and if you make it through the game without giving up, I will reward you with a prize as well," she whispered in his ear. She gave him a light kiss on the cheek.

"Ready ladies? Aim…Fire!"

The room erupted in squeals of delight as the women began shooting their rubber bands at James' cock and balls. The impact on him was minimal, since rubber bands are not very aerodynamic, their speed was reduced over the distance of a few feet to a bearable sensation. Still, James twitched and jerked as the bands smacked against his genitals. The activity did nothing to reduce his erection, and the impact of the rubber bands on his skin was slightly painful yet arousing.

James continued to twitch and writhe as the ladies exhausted their ammunition. Amazingly, one of the women actually managed to ring his cock with a rubber band. A cheer went up and the women applauded as the winner threw her hands up in victory. James was catching his breath and looking at his cock with a rubber band dangling from it in amazement.

The Hostess stepped forward and declared the winner. She then pulled the woman to her feet and addressed the group. "Since we have a winner, I guess I should award her prize."

The group burst into applause again.

"Your reward for winning is the object you managed to ring," the smiling Hostess said.

The winner giggled and smiled.

Taking James' cock in her hand, the Hostess said, "You may take possession of this prize for the next 30 minutes to do with as you will."

She looked at James as she said this and he beamed, this was the reward for him as well.

The winner reached over and grabbed his erect penis and stroked it a couple of times.

"I think I can find something to do with this for the next half-hour!"

The Hostess never did tell me what happened after that, but I have a vivid imagination.

Fresh as A Daisy

Some people have the impression I do nothing but CBT. I learned long ago that in medicine, like BDSM, a Specialist gets less work than a General Practitioner. Though I sincerely love CBT, I do lots of other things. I especially love any scene that involves the precise application of pain, or intense stimulation as the case may be.

One of my favorite tools is about the simplest one your can get, the clothespin. These little clips can be used almost anywhere on the body and if you use enough of them they can have a profound effect on the bottom. It is that kind of effect I love. I really get excited when I have a willing man or woman covered with hundreds of carefully placed clothespins. The physiological effect borders on the ecstatic because of the flood of endorphins released by the body, and the flow and patterns of the clothespins on the skin can be downright artistic.

I have written about using clothespins in CBT scenes before but I was talking about the traditional wooden clips with a spring holding the two slats together. As a child I remember my mother getting a small set of plastic clothespins from a local service station as a gift. That was before gas stations had loan officers and they actually competed for business.

This was a travel clothesline and the little clips were only an inch long. They were pretty lame as far as hanging clothes, so they ended up in my possession as a toy. Today, many years later, I have once again found the tiny clips. They are still being made and sold as travel accessories, and they still don't work worth a damn for hanging clothes, but as toys they are wonderful. I keep a set of 50 or so in my toy bag for special scenes.

Luckily I was having one of those scenes a few months back. It was at the regular dungeon party of the men's play group I belong to. I had a friend festooned with about a hundred regular wooden pins and he was starting to really have a good time. He was laying on a makeshift table constructed on a heavy door placed on a couple of industrial strength sawhorses.

I looked into his eyes and saw the familiar glow of an endorphin rush. He was flying and I felt a little guilty pushing him further… but only a little guilty. As I watched his reaction, I let my fingers trail down the pins along his arms and his chest. The stimulation of moving them made them all the more painful. When my fingers reached his abdomen, I continued down until I was teasing his genitals. He moaned a few times, but was far too involved with the pain of the pins to become aroused much.

I played with his semi-hard cock for a few minutes before pulling out the plastic box containing the travel clothespins. I opened the box and pulled one of the bright plastic pins out. It was almost day-glow yellow. I held it in front of his face for a minute until he focused on it and then opened and closed the pin's jaws a few times.

His eyes opened wider and he realized that I intended to use the pin and probably more of them somewhere "private". All he could do was whistle a little faint sound. The melody sounded more like the shrill cry of a bomb being dropped. He ended the whistle with a guttural impression of an explosion.

From that and his expression I knew he was ready for the next phase of the scene.

I massaged his cock a few strokes and then took the yellow pin and deftly clipped it to the remnants of foreskin surrounding his glans (the head of the penis). He winced, but didn't protest, so I continued. I added another yellow clip on the opposite side of the first, just clipping the foreskin and not the cock-head.

I am a firm believer in symmetry in a scene. It helps the bottom anticipate what is going to happen, balances the energy of the scene and looks prettier than an asymmetrical mess. I put that preference down to my mild case of obsessive compulsion.

I waited for him to process the pain from the second clip before adding another. I have found that setting a pace that allows a little adjustment to the sensations helps the bottom endure the pain better. I began to add another pin beside the first one, paused for him to process and continued again. The pace was natural and steady and soon his entire foreskin, such as it was, was lined with yellow miniature clothespins.

There must have been about 20 pins spaced close together hanging in a circle from the skin around his glans. They looked very nice, like a circle of sunshine around his cock.

Once the last pin was in place, I looked back to his face. He was smiling a little, but I suspected that was from the endorphins.

"Well your cock looks so very nice now," I told him. "I think you might like to see it."

He giggled nervously. " I don't know about that," he said. "I don't think I can sit up far enough to see it right now."

"That's why I brought this," I replied as I pulled a small hand mirror from my bag.

I handed him the mirror so he could use it to see his cock. I held his penis firmly in my right fist, the skin pushed up causing the pins to stand on end, sticking up vertically.

"Oh my God!" he whimpered.

"Wait just a minute," I told him. "It's a magic trick."

He looked at me with a puzzled expression and I explained.

"It's not a cock, it's a flower. Look," I said.

He positioned the mirror again and looked at his penis. As he did I slowly pulled the foreskin back down the shaft. This action caused the tiny yellow clothespins to open up, making a bright collar around his cock resembling a daisy.

"You made it bloom!" He laughed and then put the mirror down.

"Pretty isn't it?" I waited a few seconds and then finished my thought. "But it will be even more fun when I pluck it."

His eyes snapped open and his face lit up with a combination of terror and amusement.

"You aren't going to pull my dick off!"

"Nope just the petals of the flower."

As I removed each pin, being careful to avoid cutting his tender skin with the plastic edges, I lapsed into the children's rhyme. "He loves it." I pulled off the first pin to a sharp intake of breath from him.

"He loves it not!" Another pin came off and this time he whimpered. The skin being compressed by the pins contained lots of nerve endings and the extreme pressure made those nerves fire off signals to the brain of pain. That signal, along with the ones from the other pins on his body was what started the endorphin pump going. That chemical was the body's way of neutralizing pain. It is a natural opiate. Clothespins also cut off the blood flow to the skin they pinch. Cutting off that flow eventually deadens the nerve and the signals stop. The nerve goes to sleep, much like your arm might go to sleep if you lay on it wrong. Removing the pins lets the blood rush back in and along with that blood, the pain returns really fast!

"He loves it!" I pulled off another pin. "He loves it NOT!" The next pin must have been directly on a nerve because he yelped with pain, bucking off the table a little. I waited for it to subside and then continued.

Once the last pin was removed, he was giddy from all the endorphins. As I pulled the foreskin back down his cock and squeezed it, the pain cycle started all over again and he involuntarily called me at least a half dozen unflattering names.

I then removed the remaining pins from his body and held him close while he recovered from the sensations. His breathing returned to normal and I could feel him relaxing from the tension he had held during the scene.

This part of the play is often called aftercare, but I consider it as vital to a scene as anything else. It's a chance for the bottom and the Top to connect both physically and emotionally as the sensations of the scene are fully processed. For a Top it is a chance to literally feel the energy generated from the scene. The shivers and shakes of a bottom's body as he or she comes down from the peak experience of a really good scene is profound. It is one of the things I relish as a Top.

When my friend finally had returned to a semblance of normal, he pulled away and looked into my face.

"How do you feel?" I asked him.

"Fresh as a daisy," he said.

Arts & Crafts

Sometimes finding the right toy is impossible. That's where having a little skill and ingenuity comes in handy. I am by no means a great builder or woodworker, but I manage to cobble together toys for myself when I can't find what I am looking for.

One such toy came from a special request. I used to attend parties at a private home of a couple I knew. They had a small playroom built into their garage/basement and the parties were always fun. Though there were not many guests compared to some of the large play parties I have been to, the level of play was good.

My friends had a few ground rules, like most play spaces, and some of them reflected the personal tastes and quirks of the owners of the home. For example, Mary had no problem with any kind of activity with the exception of a couple. First, no watersports or scat was allowed. This was a common enough prohibition. The second was no blood or piercing. That made doing some things difficult if not impossible.

Mary was a friend and the hostess of the party so I respected Mary's rules. One night I had a couple ask me about doing a "butterfly board" at the next party. The husband was eager to try it and his wife wanted to watch. That was going to be a problem with Mary's rules, so I told them that perhaps I could come up with a suitable alternative. Something that would have a similar effect and sensation without any blood or piercing involved. The couple agreed and we set a date to play at the following party.

That gave me about a month to come up with a solution to the problem. With a little think-time, a few trips to the hardware store and some work, here is what I came up with.

The feeling of having a butterfly done to your scrotum is interesting. Your skin is being stretched out along the surface of the board and you are being pierced numerous times. The piercing part was out of the question, so I developed an alternative. Surprisingly, the non-piercing version is more painful than the real thing!

I used tiny alligator clips to attach the skin of the scrotum and stretch it on the board. These were not the kind with sharp teeth that you might find at a hardware store, but a flat bladed version that only compressed the skin and would not pierce it. The actual size of the surface that pinched the skin was very close to the area of the tiny travel clothespins I use in CBT scenes. The difference is that the alligator clips are meant for holding securely to a circuit board, and so they have a lot more spring-power. Because the surface area being pinched is so small, the blood flow is never completely closed off as with full-sized clothespins and clamps, therefore the pain never stops. With a piercing, once the needle has gone through the skin, the sensation is pretty much over.

Since the board did not need to be soft enough for a needle to penetrate, I used a piece of Plexiglas. This plastic was about 3/16" thick by 14" square and was easily worked with traditional wood working tools. I used a circle-saw intended for making holes in doors for doorknobs to cut the main hole. With gentle steady pressure and a fast drill, the hole cut cleanly and without cracking the Plexiglas. I then took abrasive and smoothed the edges of the hole until they were rounded and would pose no danger of cutting the skin.

I attached a small leather strap above the hole, to use to affix the bottom's penis, in a position out of the way of the rest of the action. It also gave me a chance to incorporate at least a little leather in the toy. It's my fetish you know!

For the stretching part, I attached the alligator clips to small pieces of bead-chain and screwed the loose ends to the board in a radial pattern surrounding the main hole. These were fastened to the Plexiglas with small bolts. Also attached to the bolts were 1" bulldog clips. These would be used to clip any slack in the chain and stretch the skin.

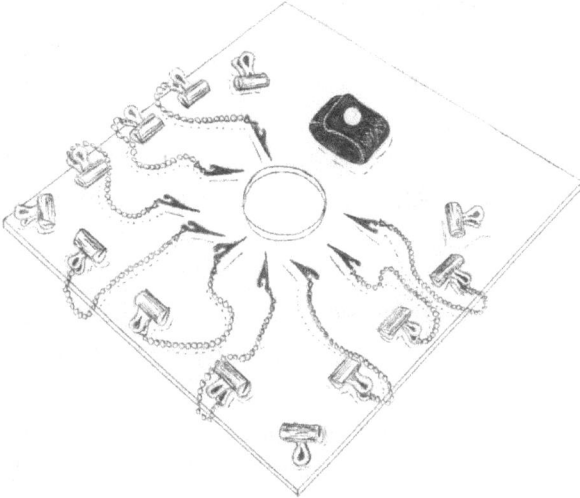

Before the party, I decided to try the toy out. Since I didn't have any willing bottom handy that afternoon, I stepped up to the plate myself. I often test toys on myself to understand what they feel like. I sincerely believe if the Top doesn't know what something feels like, he is flying blind. This doesn't mean I had to enjoy the experience, or do a complete scene, but at least I wanted to know it was safe before subjecting a volunteer to the role of crash test dummy.

I have a big mirror in the dressing area just off the bedroom. It often comes in handy for these kinds of experiments. I undressed and stood before the mirror with my new toy. The thought of it excited me to the point that I was glad I included the cock-strap. It held my erection out of the way so I could see what I was doing with the clips. Also it helped hold the whole thing on while I worked. In practice, I would have the bottom lying on his back and gravity would act as a third hand.

I took the first clip and attached it to the skin of my scrotum. This was definitely more painful than a needle! Once I caught my breath, I stretched the chain out and clamped the slack with the bulldog clip. I did three more clips before I was satisfied it would be a viable alternative to a butterfly board. Also, the pain was pretty intense and I was standing up trying to juggle everything, so I opted to end the experiment at four clips. I was also getting high from the experience and didn't want to be standing too long.

I cleaned the board up using spray window cleaner and packed it away for the party. Another advantage of Plexiglas for a toy is its ease in cleaning.

That night the couple I had negotiated the scene with was at Mary's house for the monthly party. Since there were so many people who wanted to see the new scene, we staged it in Mary's living room, using her coffee table as the location. The man bottoming for me was nervous, he had never played with a gay man or for that matter any man before, but with a little encouragement from his wife, and a few tricks of my own, he "rose to the occasion".

Once his cock was strapped down and his balls extended through the Plexiglas board, I began methodically attaching the clips to his skin. I worked slowly, much the way I would when using real needles. The pace is important, to allow the bottom to adjust to the pain and sensations. Finding the right speed is a talent learned from experience. A Top has to learn to read the bottom's body language and watch carefully how he is reacting to the sensations. For me, a good scene is like a story. It has a beginning where the characters are introduced, a middle where the plot takes shape and a conclusion where things are resolved. I try to make sure that the bottom can follow the "storyline" of the scene. It avoids bottoms becoming confused and panicking. If the bottom can clearly understand the "storyline", he can better enjoy and process the sensations. That doesn't mean there can't be surprises; if a scene is too predictable it can be boring.

As I slowly attached each clip, the skin of his scrotum was stretched out in a pattern that resembled a butterfly, pinned in a collector's box. That's where the name came from. His wife brought a camera, and since she had gotten permission from Mary to take pictures of the scene, she got some souvenirs to put in their kinky album. (Photography at most BDSM events is forbidden, but sometimes you can arrange to take pictures with the approval of the Host or Hostess. If you do so, try not to include anyone but the participants in your scene. Privacy in these cases is very important since there are many people who are not "out" with their kink.)

As I continued to add clips, the man's breathing was becoming erratic. I waited for him to grow accustomed to the pain. It took a while, since I had eleven clips on his scrotum. I only had twelve of them on the toy. Finally he calmed a bit and I added the last clip. Hs wife was delighted and took several snapshots of the arrangement. He beamed in pride at having been able to endure the ordeal and I felt sure he would be rewarded sufficiently later.

As I previously mentioned, since the alligator clips don't fully block the blood supply, the nerves being affected by the clips never stop sending their messages to the brain. In other words, hey hurt like hell. That is why in this case, unlike clothespins, there is not as much of a secondary scene when the clips are removed. With clothespins, removing them is almost as painful as putting them on. With these little clips from hell, removing them is a little painful, but mainly a relief!

After a few minutes, I began removing the clips and the tortured skin of his scrotum began to retract. Little square marks were evident on the skin where the clamps had been, these tiny symmetrical pairs of red spots would go away in a few hours, but for the time being they were fascinating to his wife who couldn't resist feeling them. Not surprisingly, they were tender, and her fingers set off a wave of groaning in her husband that both she and I found delightful.

By the time the last clip was removed, his cock had shriveled to a point where it slipped from the strap without being released. Sometimes, even for the most serous masochist, the sensations overwhelm the sex drive.

I examined his balls to make sure there wasn't any broken skin, and then just to make sure I sprayed them with a mist of rubbing alcohol. The spray evaporated quickly, the cooling made the skin of the scrotum contract and soon his balls were tight and close to his body. Again he moaned, and I smiled at his wife.
"I think he will fully recover," I told her.

"Yes," she said, "but I can always show him the pictures if he forgets."

A Pressing Engagement

Last year, my truck was vandalized and the radio was stolen. More importantly, the thieves took my toy box. Since it was in reality a rolling toolbox, the kind used by mechanics to hold their expensive tools, the thieves probably saw a chance for a quick buck at the pawnshop. I can imagine their surprise when inside they found, alligator clips, clothespins, cock rings, butt plugs, ball stretchers, electro-torture devices, and at least a dildo or two.

Unless pawnshops have changed a lot recently, I suspect the whole box ended up in a Dumpster somewhere and is now parts of a land fill. My biggest relief was that my floggers and whips had been removed for cleaning and where hanging in my house. I have at least three or four of Janet Heartwood's floggers and several others made by close friends that are irreplaceable.

Still it did wipe out my CBT toy collection and I have spent the better part of a year replacing them. That's a double-edged sword in itself. It costs a lot to refill the toy box, but I get to shop for new toys!

One of the toys that are hardest to replace was a ball vice. There are commercially available ones, but I had made my own and didn't relish doing it again.

The vice consisted of a rather simple workbench vice, the kind installed on the edge of a worktable to hold wood or other material in a vertical position for carpentry. The addition of two sheets of Plexiglas that extend about 6 inched above the vice make it a great CBT toy. These plastic sheets are ½" thick and have smooth polished edges to prevent any unwanted cuts.

My version has bolts that hold the plastic sheet to the vice. The heads of these bolts protrude a little into the space between the sheets and prevent the vice from fully closing.

The gap is about 3/8" and I consider it a safety measure. It prevents the vice from fully closing and that gap keeps me from smashing a partner's testicles into mincemeat. Did I mention that I put this on guy's nuts?

Well, after I rebuilt the ball vice, I felt I really needed to try it out, so I called my friend Dennis. He is a delightfully twisted Daddy in the community who has an occasional bottom urge when it comes to CBT. He also is a good enough friend that I can try out toys with and not worry about having to keep up any Top persona while fumbling with a new gadget. Essentially, Dennis and I experiment together and that is pretty much the scene. He enjoys the CBT experience and I get to learn how to use the new toys and get really good feedback from another Top as I do.

I packed up my vice and headed over to Dennis' place to see how well it worked. Since I had already built one, this wasn't much of a test, but it never hurts to have a trial run before you embarrass yourself in a public setting.

Dennis greeted me at the door with his characteristic good-natured smile. We adjourned to his living room and he offered me a drink. I settled in and sipped the cold soda he brought me and gave him the full story of the stolen toy box. The details about explaining to the police what was in the tool chest gave him a good laugh. It seems the local police have no idea what BDSM means. I finally settled on "sex toys and whips and chains" as a description of the chest's contents. That got a sudden expression of comprehension from the officer who showed up to take the report. He didn't press for any more details after that.

I opened the cardboard box containing the vice and showed it to Dennis. He was suitably impressed.

"Looks really nice," he said. "You made this yourself?"

"Sure did," I replied. "Amazing what you can do with a drill and a table saw. And about three hours of polishing the rough edges off."

"Well, " he said getting up from the sofa, "let's try it out."

With that he began removing his clothes. That was all the negotiation we needed to proceed. Dennis and I had played many times and both of us were fully aware of our limits and abilities. Moreover, this really wasn't going to be a "scene" as such; we were just a couple of Tops "experimenting".

Once Dennis was undressed, he laid down on the floor. I brought the vice over and knelt beside him. Dennis had a fairly normal sized cock, but his balls are really big, and they make great toys for someone who enjoys CBT. Additionally, he enjoys the special kinds of sensations CBT brings. Did I mention he is a pain pig as well?

I cranked the vice open by rotating the lever on its side. Once the Plexiglas sheets were about two inches apart I positioned the vice on Dennis' legs. One sheet lay across his legs, and I put his balls between it and the opposing plastic sheet. The crank faced up.

I told him to hold his cock out of the way, toward his abdomen as I began to tighten the vice. The great thing about the Plexiglas is that as the balls are squeezed, you can actually watch what's happening. The skin flattens out on the clear plastic and you can watch it change color as pressure is applied. It really is a visual treat. It also lets you see what is going on so you don't damage the testicles. Breaking your toys means you won't have them to play with again!

Another trick I use with this gadget to assure that the testicles are not damaged is I insert my thumb between the sheets as I tighten them. Once I feel the pressure on my thumb seems tight I know I am reaching the limit of safe compression on the balls.

Dennis closed his eyes and began to make a soft moaning sound. I could tell he had gotten into the headspace he needed to bottom and was experiencing the sensations fully. He is vocal, and that is one of the great things about playing with him. I can get clear signals as to how the scene is progressing without having to rely on body language too much. A stoic bottom is very hard to play with. I prefer the noisy type; they let me know I am doing a good job.

As I tightened the vice a few more twists, he groaned. I took this to mean he wanted to slow down, though my thumb had not yet been squeezed very tightly, I paused letting him process the sensation. I noticed his cock and gotten considerably larger as the pressure was applied. Funny how some people respond to pain?

"Want another turn?" I asked him.

He nodded and smiled a little.

I slowly turned the crank on the vice another turn, then paused. Dennis groaned again and his breathing became faster. I watched his cock twitching with each breath. Looking at his balls through the plastic of the vice they resembled a couple of fried eggs.

"Another turn?"

He nodded again. This time he held his breath waiting for it.

As I turned the handle one more time I felt the plastic jaws of the vice tightening on my thumb. I could still pull my thumb out with a little effort, but I knew I had reached the limit of what I wanted to do to his nuts.

Once his breathing slowed, I looked at Dennis and told him that his nuts looked pretty scary. His eyes opened and he promptly sat up as much as he could to look at the vice. His eyes widened like saucers as he saw his balls flattened against the Plexiglas jaws of the vice.

"Damn, that's hot!"

I nodded in agreement as I watched him start stroking his cock. The sight of his nuts in the heavy vice was a real turn on to Dennis and he had no problem showing it. He stroked his hard cock with a purpose.

"You like seeing your nuts in my vice don't you, boy?"

"Yes sir," Dennis replied. Though we were both Tops, he enjoyed falling into "boy mode" when we played. Dennis was old guard leather, meaning he had come from a tradition of coming through the ranks. He had been someone's boy and even a slave at one time before assuming the role of Top. It is why he was so good at training boys, since he had been one himself.

"You gonna make that hard cock shoot for me boy?" I taunted. "Make it cum to show me how much you like my new toy?"

"Yes sir, if it pleases you, sir"

My own dick was rigid and pressing hard against my jeans as I watched him stroke. He never took his eyes off the vice on his nuts as he jacked his cock.

"Cum for me, boy," I said in my best Top voice, and involuntarily rubbed the bulge in my jeans.

His eyes rolled back in his head as he stiffened and began to shake. AT that moment his cock erupted with a stream of cum that shot all the way up to his chin.

"Aww fuck yes!" Dennis cried.

He continued to jack his spurting dick a few more times, drenching his chest with cum. His head dropped back to the floor and he lay there panting. I slowly began opening the vice and letting the pressure off his spent nuts.

I waited for his breathing to return to normal before I spoke.

"Damn boy," I said. "That was quite a load we squeezed out of your balls."

He opened his eyes and looked down at the mess on his chin and chest.

"Wonder how much we can get out of yours?" Dennis smiled.

"I guess we are going to have to find out." I said and began unbuckling my belt.

Fire and Ice

Sometimes the best toys are the simplest ones. I get a chance to watch a lot of CBT scenes at the many events I attend and I always am amazed at the creativity and imagination shown by people when it comes to toys. As I mentioned earlier, a lot of really good stuff comes from hardware, kitchen or specialty stores that don't sell sex toys, at least they don't think they do! These "pervertables" as folks in the leather community have come to call them make up much of my toy bag. It's always nice to find a new one or to see someone using a common object in a different way. The following story uses one "genuine" CBT toy and the simplest of pervertables I can thing of.

I was attending a week long combination camp out and play party deep in the woods of Michigan where annually an extended family of leathermen gather to play, schmooze and carouse. It's one of the best places to see really intense play, and one of my favorite spots to learn from the best players in the country.

In one of the areas reserved for more intimate play, such as CBT and medical scenes, I watched a couple of guys use little more than a one basic toy and have a very hot scene.

Gary, a middle-aged man about my height, and sporting a salt and pepper beard had just bound his boy, Mark to an inclined table. Mark was a good looking man of about 40 and he took care of his body. He had a few tribal tattoos and pierced nipples, not uncommon for the group of men attending the event. He was secured with leather wrist cuffs attached to the top of the table, stretching his body downward along the table, and exposing his ample cock and balls for the scene. Mark's feet and legs were strapped down with leather belts that ran through slots in the inclined table.

Gary was putting a leather CBT toy on Mark. The leather shops call these gadgets the "Gates of Hell", and they come in both metal and leather versions. They consist of a series of rings attached to a strap. The biggest ring is designed to go around the cock and balls exactly like a cock ring. The additionally rings go around the shaft of the penis and terminate in a small ring that can be used to attach the toy to either a weight or a leash. Personally, I have little use for the metal ones since I haven't had much success in using them. Something about the cold metal not being conducive to an erection and without an erection the whole thing just hangs there like a kinky wind chime.

The leather version works the same way, but has a series of leather straps that snap around the cock and balls and the shaft of the penis. This works much better since it has some ability to adjust for different size organs and is not COLD! Gary's was the leather kind and from the looks of Mark's rigid cock it was working just fine.

Once secured, Gary tool a length of nylon cord and ran it through the ring on th eend of the "gates" and then up to Mark's left nipple ring. He threaded the cord through the ring and the over to the right one and back down to the "gates" making a triangle of cord that pulled Mark's hard cock against his body. The tension on the nipple rings also added to the sensation.

Gary teased Mark for a while, stroking his leather-ringed cock and then pulling the cord to exert tension on his nipples. He had tightened the cord to just the right point where every time Mark's cock jumped, it tugged a little at his nipples.

Gary paused a few seconds and reached into a pocket in his vest. He pulled out a couple of cigars. Looking toward me, he offered me one. I never refuse a good cigar, and these were my favorite, Romeo y Julieta, made in Cuba! Did I mention Gary and Mark were from Canada, where Cuban cigars are common?

Well after we had lit up, Gary moved back to Mark and drew very close to his face. I could see in Mark's eyes the sexual tension. Gary paused a few seconds and the slowly exhaled a stream of thick cigar smoke directly into Mark's face. At that moment I saw Mark's cock twitch and bounce. Obviously he liked the smell!

Gary puffed a few more times and then kissed Mark deeply before moving back to his cock and balls. He took the cigar from his lips, after puffing it again, and moved it closer to Mark's exposed scrotum. As it neared I watched Mark struggle a little. Gary brought the gray ash at the tip of the cigar within a half and inch of Mark's smooth shaved balls. Holding it there as the heat from the smoldering tobacco began affecting Mark's skin. It wasn't enough to burn him, but he could feel the heat, and the body's reaction to heat is very quick and profound. It's the reaction that makes you pull your hand away from a hot stove before being burned.

Mark let out a slight moan as he began reacting to the heat of the cigar. At that moment Gary pulled the cigar back and puffed on it a couple of times. Mark looked at him with a new fire in his eyes. I saw a combination of anger, fear and pure sexual energy.

"Don't you dare touch my balls with that cigar, you bastard!" Mark spat the words out.

Gary laughed and moved to Mark's face again. He blew another mouth full of smoke at his boy then laughed with the sexiest, deepest voice I have ever heard. He smiled at me and spoke.

"I don't think this boy is in any position to make demands, do you?"

"Well," I replied, "I guess it just shows you how spunky he is."

Mark momentarily broke from the angry and frightened character he had assumed and looked at me with what I assumed was slight frustration. "Spunky?"

Normally I would never have broken the mood of a scene like that, but I knew both men very well and delighted in busting their chops occasionally. That was one of the nice things about this event. The men here were confident and rarely took themselves too seriously.

Gary laughed and the puffed again on his cigar before returning it to Mark's balls. As he brought the long great ash closer and closer to Mark's balls, mark resumed his struggling.

"Hold still boy, or I might accidentally burn you." Gary growled. "And if I burn you I don't want it to be an accident."

Mark stiffened and spat back, "Yes sir, thank you sir...bastard."

Gary chuckled again as he brought the cigar ash closer and closer to Marks balls. Suddenly he pushed the cigar directly into Mark's nuts, the gray ash leaving a smudge on his skin. Mark yelped and then panted while he processed the sensation.

Though to an outsider it might have seemed that Gary had just burned Mark's balls, in actuality he simply left a trace of ash on them. Cigar ash is a pretty good insulator, and the hottest part of the cigar was about an inch down from the tip. The burned ash was warm but not searing. Though Mark might have ended up with a slight reddening where Gary touched, it would go away in a few hours and leave no damage.

Gary moved back to Mark's face and puffed again on the cigar. This time he grabbed Mark's face and smashed his lips into his own, as he exhaled he filled Mark's mouth with smoke and kissed him deeply, invading him with his tongue. When he withdrew, Mark blew the smoke from his mouth and took a much needed breath of fresh air.

I guess I don't have to tell you that smoking is hazardous to your health. Cigar smoke is very potent and inhaling it is a bad idea. Gary and Mark both know this, and don't do it often, just once and a while in the heat of play. Both men smoke cigars, and know the risks associated with them. So much for the official disclaimer, now back to the scene.

Gary continued tormenting Mark like this for he next 20 minutes until the cigar was almost gone. By varying the distance from the skin with he hot ash, he could achieve a variety of sensations and occasionally touching Mark with the cooler ash added to the psychological effect of the scene.

As Gary took a couple of final puffs on his cigar he pulled an ice chest closer to him. Inside was a supply of soft drinks and lots of half-melted ice. Gary then moved back to Mark's ash smudged balls. Mark's cock had stayed hard throughout the ordeal giving a pretty good indication that he was enjoying the scene. Gary looked at me and motioned me over to help out. He pointed to my cigar, which was about the same length as his at this point.

"Why don't you take the right nut and I'll take the left one?" Gary suggested.

"I'd be delighted," I replied and moved my cigar closer to Mark's right ball.

Throughout the scene Mark had been spewing curses and threats at Gary, and now he turned his venom toward me. Had I not known the men, I would have questioned his behavior, but I knew Gary loved hearing Mark curse him during a scene. It got the men's adrenaline going and made the energy between them more sexual bordering on the animalistic. That energy would serve them well later when Mark and Gary returned to the privacy of their cabin for the second half of the scene.

We both moved our cigars closer and closer to Mark's scrotum. The skin of his balls seemed to contract as if trying to move away from the heat. Taking my cue from Gary I kept my cigar at the same distance as his. As we neared the skin, Mark began to moan louder. Gary looked at me and nodded. I knew what he had planned since I had seen him do this before. Just about the time the glowing end of the cigar was in contact with the skin, at his signal we both turned the cigars over and smashed the non-lit end into Marks balls.

Mark screamed in terror and shock. As far as he knew we had just snuffed our cigars out on his nuts, burning his balls in the process.

Before he could catch his breath, Gary thrust his hand into the ice chest and pulled out a hand-full of melting ice chunks. He smashed the ice directly into Mark's balls and held it there against his skin.

Mark yelled again this time even louder. To him the sensations of hot and cold had become indistinguishable and his mind expected more heat. The ice felt like hot coals to his already aroused nerve endings. He squirmed and thrashed against the bonds until Gary finally let the ice fall from his hand.

Mark's breathing returned to normal after a few minutes, while Gary caressed him and kissed his partner. I helped Gary unbuckle Mark from the inclined bondage table and made sure he didn't fall. His legs were wobbly from all the adrenaline and endorphins and he was grateful for the support.

Mark produced a scissors from his vest pocket and clipped the nylon cord, letting Mark's now softening cock fall free of the nipple bondage. Gary and I led Mark to a bench nearby. As we sat there, Mark turned to Gary and smiled.

"Damn you are a nasty bastard!"

He then kissed him and hugged him tightly. When he broke their embrace, he turned to me and smiled.

"He likes showing off," Gary said. "And when it's in front of friends, he's even more evil than normal."

I smiled at both of them as Gary leaned over to kiss me.

"Well," I said, "I am always glad to do what I can. Besides, it's about the only way I get to enjoy Cuban cigars!"

Odds and The End

Ideas for CBT can come from anywhere. As I have noted previously, the hardware store often is a place of great inspiration, but I have found nifty CBT toys at kitchen specialty stores, tack shops and even children's toy stores. All you need is an overactive imagination and a kinky sensibility to discover lots of possible gadgets that can be used in a scene.

I even find new ideas in kinky places. Last week I attended a leather swap-meet where numerous vendors were displaying their wears. At one table a woman was demonstrating what she called a Bondage Bra. It was a length of surgical tubing with adjustable loops at the ends. These were designed to fit around the breasts and the tubing looped over the neck to support them. It was a novel idea and really made a woman's breasts stand out. Her point in the invention was to have a piece of bondage gear that could be worn under street clothes. She wanted to stand next to her boss and still be in bondage. Now that's kinky!

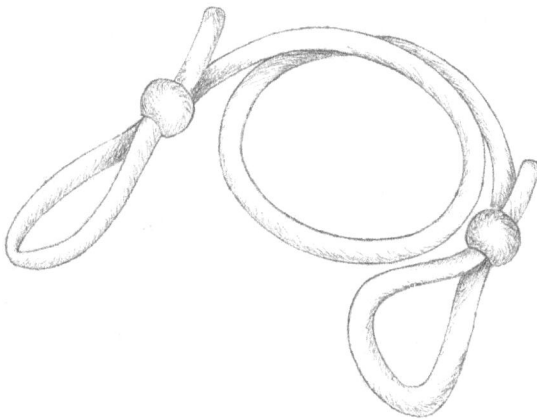

Not surprisingly, the tubing looked like it would be good for CBT as well. She and I discussed the possibilities and I purchased one of her bras for myself. So far it looks promising. The tubing works great for cock and ball bondage and the sliding beads that adjust the tension are coming in handy. I suspect before long this will be a regular part of my toy box.

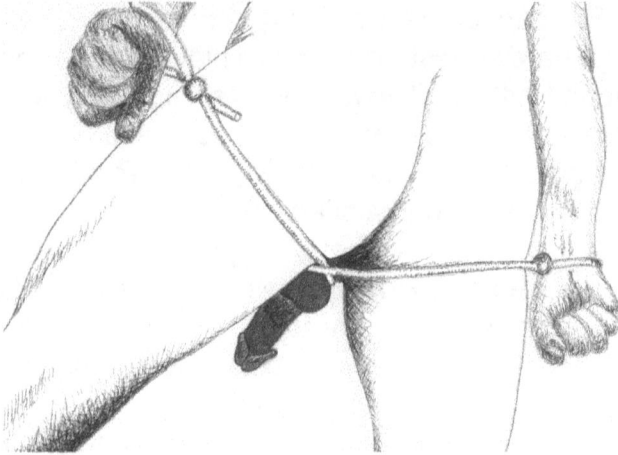

Having been an amateur magician, I still hang around magic shops occasionally as well. One little gadget I use in my lectures came from my experience as a magician. I am sure everyone has seen a performer use a version of a guillotine at some time or another. I built a miniature guillotine to use in a CBT scene. I keep it in my toy box and pull it out once I have a volunteer for a demo. Using the blade of the device to cut the end of a cigar, the bottom quickly becomes aware that the guillotine is capable of cutting.

The hole, where a full sized model would accommodate a head, is just big enough for an erect penis. I manage to get my volunteer to place his cock through the hole and I position the blade in the slot above it. Having seen it work on my cigar, an erection is usually out of the question at this point, but some twisted guys enjoy the fear.

At some point while I am talking I ask the bottom if he truly believes I would use the guillotine on his cock. Some nod while other just laugh nervously. Before I can finish assuring them that I would never do anything to harm their penis, I slam my hand down on the device sending the blade down, where it seemingly passes through their penis.

Needless to say, it's a trick. Though I won't reveal the secret, the volunteer is none the worse for wear and it makes a nice finish to a demo. The whole guillotine idea was inspired by watching a magician whose act was wild and seemingly uncontrolled. As an audience member I never knew whether to laugh or run from the theatre. That was part of his illusion. Giving me the impression that he was capable of something that would be really scary gave him an edgy appeal. The guillotine serves the same purpose for me.

As I said in my earlier book, the greatest sex organ in our body is between our ears. Imagination can make the mundane titillating. Even though the people I play with know I would never harm them, it's not a bad thing to have a little edge. For many BDSM players, a little fear is a good thing. I am not talking about real fear for personal safety, but just a hint of uneasiness that makes the experience sharper and more exciting.

The stories in this book - as in my previous book - are all true, just altered a bit for privacy. I have tried to make each clear and understandable as not only a tale of a hot scene, but somewhat instructive as well. I have tried to emphasize the safety and precautions that should be taken in each scene as well as some of the subtleties of negotiation and communications involved.

More importantly, these stories were meant to inspire the reader to create his or her own stories. Our play chronicles our journey as leatherfolk. As we share our stories with each other, we all grow in our collective experience. I know of few other communities who do this as well as we do. Sitting around a coffee table discussing scenes or chatting at a leather bar with friends, we continue to build our collective experience. Sharing my stories and those of my friends here is my contribution.

Now, go out and start collecting your own tales. Play safely, use common sense and you will find consensual partners. Whether you play with your wife, husband, significant other or just good friends, you are writing a story. I urge you to share what you learn and discover with others. To go out on a limb and paraphrase the scriptures, "don't light a lamp and put it under a basket. Put it on a lampstand, where it gives light to all who are in the house."

About the Author

Since the mid-70's Hardy has been an active in the leather community and a member of many BDSM/Fetish organizations including Dallas Motorcycle Club, Leather Rose Society, NLA-Dallas, Discipline Corps and a founding member of Inquisition-Dallas. Considering himself a "Pain Technologist" he specializes in CBT and has an unusual fondness for clips clamps and clothespins, as well as more esoteric SM play.

Professionally he is a filmmaker. His documentary on the leather lifestyle "LEATHER" has won numerous awards and appeared in festivals around the world, and his latest film, "Out of the Darkness, The Reality of SM" is currently being used by health care professionals around the world. His non-leather projects include the documentary "The Big Fair" a look inside the State Fair of Texas, which is soon to be distributed.

Outside his filmmaking, he is a gay political activist, author & speaker on aspects of the SM/Leather scene. His first book "The Family Jewels, A guide to male genital play and torment" is available at bookstores everywhere.

He was awarded NLAI's *Man of the Year* award in 1999 and in 2007 he was honored with a *Lifetime Achievement Award* from the National Leather Association International. Since April, 1995, he and his boy Patrick have been living together in Dallas with their Feline Mistresses, Elvira and Samantha and newcomer Jack-The-Cat.